THE LEARNING LOVE

HANDBOOK

A SERIES OF BOOKS FOR LEARNING THE ART OF LOVING AND INTIMACY

BOOK I

PART 1:
OPENING TO VULNERABILITY

The Way back to Self-love and Intimacy

PART 2:
LETTING GO

Recovering from Abandonment, Rejection, and Loss

ISBN: 1481076566

ISBN 13: 9781481076562

CreateSpace Independent Publishing Platform

North Charleston, South Carolina

PART 1

OPENING TO VULNERABILITY –

The Way Back to Self-Love and Intimacy

TABLE OF CONTENTS

INTRODUCTION:

With this book, we invite you to take a journey with us.

The book is meant to accompany a two-track CD, sold separately, with each track a guided meditation dealing with one of the two parts of this book.

This book is part of a series. Each book has an accompanying CD dealing with different aspects of the process of learning self-love and intimacy. The series comprises what we are calling *The Learning Love Handbook.*

This book, the first of the series, is in two parts.

Part 1 deals with opening our vulnerability.

Opening vulnerability means exposing the depth of our fears and insecurities to ourselves and to a person we become intimate with.

In our experience, this is first step in the journey of learning love.

Most of us have had difficult experiences in our past that caused us to lose trust and close our hearts.

We may have become afraid to open to another person, to life, and even to ourselves.

And in this state of closure, we may have forgotten or become too afraid to share and we may continue to create painful rejections in our lives.

However, opening our vulnerability could be perhaps the most courageous and intelligent step we can make in life because it opens us to love, and it makes us available to be loved.

Gradually, with simple tools that we outline in this series, by opening to our vulnerability, we can take the journey back to intimacy, to appreciating ourselves, and to enjoying life.

In Part 2 of this book, we address situations in our lives when we are faced with rejection, abandonment, or loss or when we feel frustrated and disappointed with a close person in our life.

We encounter these situations often especially if we choose to open and become vulnerable.

But frequently, such a situation can cause us to close again, perhaps even to lose more trust and to become bitter, angry, or depressed.

It may be a painful rejection, or the loss of someone we love, or being in a relationship that is not giving us the love we hoped for.

The second part of this book guides you to be able to use these painful experiences as opportunities for deepening and growth, toward more inner strength, confidence, and self-love.

The meditations on the CD are deep inner journeys that work with the subconscious mind to guide you to learn the tools we describe in the book.

We suggest that you listen to the meditations frequently, as they help to develop the qualities of understanding and inner space that we find so useful in our work and for ourselves.

CHAPTER 1:

WHAT IS VULNERABILITY?

There is a beautiful children's story called *The Velveteen Rabbit* by Margery Williams.

It is about a rabbit made of cloth that is given to a child for Christmas. The child plays with him for a little while, but shortly loses interest and leaves him alone because he finds his newer, fancier toys more exciting. Soon, the other toys in the child's room ignore the velveteen rabbit because he isn't an expensive toy and has no prestige. The only toy in the nursery that is nice to him is the "Skin Horse"— the wooden horse. He is the oldest toy in the room and has seen many toys come and go over the years.

One day, the Rabbit asks the horse, "What is REAL?"

"Real," answers the Horse, "is not how you are made, it's a thing that happens to you. When a child loves you for a long, long time, not just to play with, but REALLY loves you, then you become REAL."

"Does it hurt?" asks the Rabbit.

"Sometimes, but when you are Real, you don't mind being hurt," answers the Horse.

"Does it happen all at once, like being wound up," he asks, "or bit by bit?"

"It doesn't happen all at once," says the Skin Horse. "You become. It takes a long time. That's why it doesn't happen to people who break easily, or have sharp edges, or who have to be carefully kept. Generally, by the time you are Real, most of your hair has been loved off, and your eyes drop out and you get loose in the joints and very shabby. But these things don't matter at all, because once you are Real, you can't be ugly, except to people who don't understand."

The story goes on from there, and we leave it for you to read and enjoy.

Becoming real is about learning to become vulnerable again.

We are all born in a state of exquisite vulnerability.

We *feel everything.*

We are *immensely sensitive.*

Every new experience is *full of wonder,* and we are overflowing with *enthusiasm and spontaneity.*

But as we grow older, most of us slowly lose this precious state.

The joy and innocence fades, we lose much of our spontaneity, and often we become *cautious* and *mistrustful* of life and other people.

Our hearts close, our natural life energy declines. Instead of inviting newness, adventure, and growthful experiences, we *shrink* our lives and become accustomed to what is safe and familiar.

Instead of having love, we live in *isolation, conflict, disappointment,* or *depression.*

We may have had painful relationships and they have left us feeling hurt and fearful of opening again.

We may even believe that we do not deserve happiness and love in our lives, or if we do, we don't know how or where to find it.

Or we blame others or difficult circumstances in our life for our unhappiness.

Something may have died inside and lost the pure joy of living.

Why has this happened?

It happened through experiences that *damaged* our innocence and trust in people and in life.

It happened because we have been *traumatized* by challenging life experiences and by the insensitivities and lack of real love that we received.

Furthermore, we did not learn how to grow through these experiences and how to cope with the pain they bring.

We long to recover our hopefulness and joy in life, but we don't know how.

CHAPTER 2:

HOW WE LOST OUR WAY

We will start by giving you a helpful picture, a model to help you understand how we have lost our ability to love ourselves and other people deeply.

Imagine that there are three layers to your being arranged in circles, each inside the other. How we develop these three layers is an important story because it tells us much about how we are living in our lives today and why.

The Layer of Essence

The story begins when we are born, or even in the womb.

At this time, we have only one circle. This circle represents our _essence_.

It holds our basic qualities and gifts that everyone is born with. Some of these qualities are *universal to everyone*—such as lovingness, joy, enthusiasm, aliveness, and trust.

Some of the qualities in our essence are totally *unique* to us—they are our special gifts, our special flavor of interests, talents, and how our life energy naturally wishes to express itself.

We may feel this essence layer very strongly at times when we are engaged in a sport, making love, walking in nature, dancing, or involved in some other form of creative expression.

The reason we often feel joy at seeing a child in his or her natural spontaneity, enthusiasm, playfulness, sweetness, silence, and lovingness is because it reminds us of our essence.

And also, if we get to know this still-innocent and spontaneous child, we begin to sense his or her special qualities that define him or her as a unique person.

This is what we call essence.

The Layer of Wounded Vulnerability

But as the years go by, our story becomes more complicated.

For one reason or another, we leave this Garden of Eden of unspoiled innocence and trust.

Slowly, our innocence becomes jaded, our trust turns to mistrust, our spontaneity turns to fear and caution, we lose much of our original aliveness, and our confidence turns to self-doubt.

Our layer of essence becomes *covered with a layer of hurt, mistrust, shame, and fear.*

Now, we no longer have only our circle of essence. We also have a second layer covering the inner layer.

We call this layer, *"the layer of wounded vulnerability."*

In this layer, we carry profound insecurity and feelings of worthlessness. We carry fear and even frozenness (or shock) and deep hurt.

For each of us, the experiences that cause this change are different but the result is similar.

Perhaps we felt ignored, pressured, criticized, or judged.

Perhaps our sexuality and aliveness was repressed.

Perhaps we were abused with violence.

Perhaps we had to perform a role in the family such as taking care of a depressed parent.

Perhaps we had to live up to the expectations of someone.

Perhaps one of our parents was an alcoholic or abused drugs

Perhaps our parents fought and we grew up in an environment that to this small innocent child felt like a war zone.

Perhaps one or both parents were physically or emotionally absent.

When children are not treated with love and respect, they feel that this is what they deserve.

When children are unsupported in developing their natural gifts and are distracted from essence, they lose self-love and trust in people, and start to feel that this world is not a safe loving place.

Instead of seeing that the parents or caregivers have a problem, children believe that they are responsible for this unloving behavior.

Children begin to feel that they are wrong and they are bad; otherwise, they would not be treated this way.

Very early in life we may have felt capable, loving, joyful, and alive.

But after living in an unloving, sad, depressed, or violent environment we stop believing and feeling any of these wonderful qualities.

We may not even remember them anymore, as they were lost so early in our lives.

We start to believe and feel that we are defective, damaged, unworthy of love or respect, and incapable.

We are no longer connected to our gifts and special qualities that we were born with.

Sometimes we describe this second layer, the layer of wounded vulnerability, as the home of the wounded child because when we feel the fears and insecurities we carry inside, we feel very young and vulnerable—just like a small hurt child.

The Layer of Protection

But the story is not over.

Because of the hurt, insecurity, and fear that we hold in our middle layer, we have built a third layer to cover these painful feelings.

This is what we call "*the layer of protection.*"

We built this layer for many reasons.

1. We don't want to accept or feel the profound insecurity and unworthiness that we have inside, so we begin to pretend to be what we are not. We begin to *compensate, to cover up* our insecurity in order to convince ourselves and others that we are worthy and capable. We create an identity of ourselves based on achievement, image, and prestige, and then we begin to believe this is who we are.

2. We don't want to accept or feel the hurts from past experiences in childhood, adolescence, or later in life. So we cover our pain with addictions, distractions, and unhealthy relationships.

3. We don't want to allow people to hurt, reject, or abuse us again, so we close our doors to closeness and intimacy. If we do open them again, we often do this from our wounded child, who has the fantasy that the other person or people will be totally sensitive, respectful, and considerate.

This layer of protection is our armor.

It has served a good purpose; it has been our survival.

It is good to know that we can protect ourselves when we need to and we can avoid people and situations that are unhealthy or harmful.

Each one of us has his or her own *style* of protection.

- Some of us get very *angry* when we feel someone is insensitive, distant, unappreciative, unsupportive, or disrespectful in even the smallest way. Our relating becomes full of fight and conflict.

- Some of us become very *detached or removed* and *we space out when we feel overwhelmed.*

- Some of us *use our minds* as a way of staying closed, trying to figure things out, hiding behind ideas.

- We can become *pleasers, compliant,* and *submissive* so no one will be angry with us—a good boy or girl who obeys the rules and does what is expected of him or her.

- Some of us are focused on being in *power* and *control,* or feeling *superior* or more *spiritual.*

- We may protect ourselves by *giving up, sabotaging,* or playing the *victim.*

- We can be a *rescuer* and feel needed and important because we are helping people.

- We can be a chronic *complainer,* finding faults in our partner or friends.

- We can remain *distracted with addictions.*

These are all ways to not feel vulnerable.

Unfortunately, our protection is no longer a conscious choice based on situations in our present life.

It has become *unconscious, habitual,* and *automatic.*

It is based on what we project on our lives today because of experiences from the past.

We live in our layer of protection like a robot, reacting to life, people, and ourselves today from emotional imprints from our past. We are not seeing life, other people, or even ourselves clearly.

Most of us live in the layer of protection almost all the time. We are used to it. It is familiar, makes us feel safe, and gives us an identity.

Our thoughts and attitudes toward ourselves, people, and life in general are defined by protection.

"It is not safe to really open again."

"People have to be sensitive, loving, and respectful if I am going to open."

"Most people cannot really be trusted."

"I have to be strong, successful, and attractive to get love and respect."

"I have to pretend to be strong, successful, and attractive to get love and respect."

"I cannot show my fears, insecurities, or weaknesses."

"I cannot admit to myself or to anyone else that I am afraid or insecure."

"Weak people are losers."

"I have to fight or people will take advantage of me."

"It is better to be alone than to get hurt by someone."

The problem is that when we are in this space of protection without realizing it, how it feels, and where it comes from, we can stay here forever—safe but isolated, lonely, unnourished, bitter, depressed, living with low energy, angry, and deeply unhappy.

In protection, we make our lives into a fight, a complaint, a drama, and a tragedy.

Exercise: Understanding the Three Layers

Imagine that you are standing in the center of a circle.

This circle is composed of an inner circle (where you are standing), a middle circle, and an outer circle.

Now, imagine that you are stepping into the outer circle.

This is your circle of protection.

Take a moment to feel the quality of energy in this circle.

In this circle, you can feel how you protect yourself from anyone threatening you from the outside.

Allow yourself to feel this quality of protection.

Perhaps it feels a bit tense in your belly or tight in your chest.

Perhaps there is stiffness in your shoulders or your back.

Perhaps you feel that you are holding your breath.

In protection, we are shut down from our feelings, and our attention is on people and events outside.

We each have our own style, and each of us can use many different ways of protecting and defending ourselves.

Perhaps you fight, attack, or push back when you feel someone is approaching you in a disrespectful way.

Perhaps you are very quick to react in anger. If that is the case, just allow yourself to feel that energy.

Perhaps you defend yourself by being nice, pleasing, compliant, or submissive. Perhaps your style is to smile and present the image of a "good" person that people will like.

Perhaps you want to be nice so that people will not be angry.

Or perhaps when you feel threatened or unsafe, you try to smooth things over. If this is a part of your style of protection, allow yourself to feel the quality of this energy.

Perhaps your style of protection includes being spaced out, not present, absent-minded, dreamy, or removed.

Perhaps you deal with situations that are stressful by becoming forgetful or confused.

Perhaps you protect by avoiding situations where you might feel unsafe, challenged, insecure, or afraid by attempting to figure things out.

The energy of protection is compulsive, frantic, vigilant, rapid, and automatic. And paradoxically, when we are collapsing or giving up, we are also in the layer of protection because we are choosing not to engage in life.

Take some moments to feel this layer of protection; it is a crucial part of your life.

Now, imagine that you are taking a step back and entering the middle layer of the circle.

This is the layer of wounded vulnerability.

This is where we hold our hurt—the hurts in the heart—the pain of all the times we feel and have felt misunderstood, judged, not appreciated, betrayed, and rejected.

Take some time to feel the hurt in the heart.

It is also the place where we hold our deep insecurities, our shame, our feelings of not being good enough, of not living up to expectations—those of others or our own.

This is where we may feel worthless, useless, and profoundly inadequate.

We may even feel that we are nobody and cannot imagine how anyone could love us.

It is rare that we allow ourselves to feel the depth of our shame.

This is also the layer where we hold fear, terror, and even shock.

Most of us are not even vaguely aware of how deep our fears are.

We seldom take the time to feel or accept our fear and shock.

This is all part of the middle layer.

Take a few moments to feel this layer of wounded vulnerability.

We will be spending more time understanding this layer as we go along in the book.

Now, finally, imagine that you are taking another step back, right into the center of the circle.

This is the layer of essence.

In this circle, you can have a direct experience with your authentic, wonderful, unique, special, gifted self.

Take some precious moments to feel this layer.

Breathe deeply.

Maybe you notice that you are relaxing...that some of the pressure is melting away.

In our essence there is no comparison, no competition, no judging—just a deep relaxation into your being, in this moment.

Many of us have forgotten about this part of ourselves.

In the essence layer, we relax and enjoy life and ourselves as we are.

We reconnect with our being.

CHAPTER 3:

WHY IS IT SO IMPORTANT TO OPEN OUR VULNERABILITY AGAIN?

Most of us have built our lives around protection.

At first, this protection was our survival, but now we use it to avoid feeling fear or pain. It not only keeps other people from coming close to us, it also keeps us from feeling ourselves.

And when we avoid feeling the fear and pain that we have buried inside, we are cut off from a big part of our life energy; we pay a heavy price.

We may not realize that we are living lives of protection, but it shows itself in the way we are living our lives and the way people respond to us.

For instance:

Alicia does not want to feel alone or risk angering her husband, so she is compliant and submissive. She has become his emotional slave.

Robert does not want to grow up and become a responsible man. He converts every woman he has been with into his mother. He is reckless with finances, expects his girl friends to cook and clean up after him, and waits for them to arrange times together. Eventually the women get tired and leave him for another man.

Steve does not want to feel or admit his insecurity as a man. Instead, he has short affairs, impressing women with his money and importance. He complains that all women are superficial and use him for his money.

Anna insists she is unhappy because she cannot find the man of her dreams, but she cannot see that her high expectations and demands push men away.

When things don't go his way and he feels helpless, Matthew gets irritated and blames his wife. He cannot understand why she is not interested in making love with him.

When Thomas feels hurt, rather than feel and share his feelings, he shuts down and withdraws for months at a time.

Catherina does not want to feel how much anger she still has with her father for abusing her physically and sexually. Instead, she puts her rage on her husband and criticizes him endlessly.

In all of these examples, the person is compensating for fears and insecurities that he or she does not want to face, and as a result, creating great suffering for him or herself.

If we stay closed, in our protection, we are reinforcing our negative beliefs. People cannot feel us, touch our hearts, or come close to us.

If we do let someone close, but we stay in our protection, eventually we are going to reject that person or complain when he or she is not as we would like.

In our protection, we believe that other people should make us happy.

Or we believe that life is against us, that we do not deserve happiness, and we might as well give up.

We constantly check to see if the other person or the situation offers the opportunity for us to get what we want without rejection, disrespect, or hurt.

We are waiting for the other person to put down his or her guard first.

We may even try compulsively to fix or control our environment and the people around us so that we won't get hurt.

But these efforts don't work.

It makes us tense and exhausted and ultimately very lonely.

The only way out of this hell is to open to our vulnerability again, and that means to open to our hurt, insecurity, and fears inside.

That means stepping from our layer of protection into our layer of wounded vulnerability.

Exercise: Noticing how we may be living in our protection and the price we pay

Take a moment to consider your life.

In what way do you notice that you are engaging in some of the roles or behaviors that make up the layer of protection?

- Being a habitual rescuer?

- Needing to be in control?

- Raging or being chronically irritable?

- Pulling away and becoming uncommunicative?

- Being habitually nice, compliant, and submissive?

- Playing the teacher or the guru?

- Spacing out?

- Distracting with drugs, alcohol, TV, or the Internet?

What is the price that you pay in these cases?

CHAPTER 4:

WHY WE RESIST FEELING VULNERABLE AGAIN

O ne of the most basic needs that we all have is to feel that we are capable of dealing with life's challenges.

We want to feel powerful and to feel that we can master situations that life brings.

And one of the most disagreeable feelings for most people is to feel weak and helpless.

We don't want people to have power over us.

We don't want to feel that we can't conquer our difficulties.

We don't want to surrender to our fears and insecurities—or perhaps admit that we even have fears and insecurities.

And there is also another reason that we resist opening our hearts and feeling vulnerable.

Many of us would like to idealize our childhoods.

We want to believe that our parents were loving and supportive and did a good job raising us.

We don't want to have any bad feelings towards them.

But if we are not able to feel the hurts inside for the way things were, we cannot learn to love ourselves again.

Then we keep feeling responsible for whatever happened.

A healthier approach to looking at our past is to honor the love and support we did receive, but also to recognize the ways that we did not get what we needed.

In order to heal and bring back our life energy, we need to come out of denial of our childhood traumas and feel the pain we went through.

Finally, there is a third reason we would like not to feel our vulnerability.

We don't want to be hurt again.

A big part of us inside says, "I will not be vulnerable again. If I am vulnerable, people will take advantage of me. I do not want to be hurt again."

We want to avoid any situation where we might get abused or rejected.

This wound is very deep.

For these reasons, we feel much safer if we keep our armor up.

We don't want to be hurt again because it was so painful to be abused and not be able to do anything about it.

In fact, we would like to avoid our vulnerability altogether.

So we search for ways to feel happy without having to be vulnerable.

We look for things that can give us instant pleasure in the hope that this will make us happy.

Drugs, alcohol, sex, shopping, entertainment, and even sports or strong exercise can all offer us quick enjoyment without requiring us to open our hearts and our fears of being hurt again.

Or we may become absorbed with work, the Internet, or any other distraction—anything that can give us a taste of essence without having to feel vulnerable.

And if we get proficient at anything—sports, playing music, or some other hobby—we may become very attached to it because it creates a feeling of aliveness and bring us into the moment.

Falling in love can also be a direct path from protection to essence.

A new relationship is like a drug.

All of a sudden, we are full of those wonderful feelings again and we feel that from one day to the next, our lives have changed.

We have love, companionship, sex, aliveness, and joy, and we believe that we never have to be alone again. We have found the one we are waiting for, longing for, hoping for.

Then we are deeply disappointed when things don't work out the way we expected.

When we fall in love, we believe that we are vulnerable and open.

It certainly feels that way.

But our vulnerability does not really get tested until later.

It only becomes real once we have accepted the other person for who he or she is.

Prior to that, we were living in a fantasy.

All of these strategies are ways to avoid feeling vulnerable.

They are shortcuts to happiness that do not give us what we are really looking for: love, happiness, peace of mind, and deep inner relaxation. To obtain these, there are no shortcuts.

The path toward real vulnerability means having to face the pain of our loss of innocence.

Our vulnerability is no longer the free and open vulnerability of an innocent child.

Now it is the vulnerability of a person who has been deeply wounded and traumatized.

When we feel our hearts, we may often feel that they are aching or that they are quite numb.

Why is this so?

It is because our hearts feel the pain of a child who was often not treated with respect and love.

It is the pain of a child who often did not get his or her basic needs met for protection, support, guidance, warmth, appreciation, and acceptance.

It is the pain of a child who no longer trusts that if he or she opens again, it will be safe and rewarding.

We ask ourselves, "Why should I open if once again there is no one there who listens and understands?"

"Why should I open if I am only going to get hurt and abandoned again?"

"It is better to stay closed and safe."

"It is better to keep things as they are because at least I know that I can manage like this."

To open to this vulnerability means to feel the pain of a child who felt betrayed, hurt, misunderstood, ignored, unloved, pressured, or even abused.

All of these feelings are uncomfortable.

If we allow ourselves to open to our vulnerability again, we will have to feel all the pain that we have repressed.

We will have to feel the terror of being helpless to defend ourselves against disrespect, humiliation, violence, and emotional abuse.

Exercise: A Meditation on Two Parts of You

Imagine that there are two parts of you.

One part of you is used to a familiar feeling of protection and a certain level of safety.

This part of you has become somewhat comfortable with your life as it is because it is predictable and secure.

This part of you does not want to disturb things because change can be frightening.

Take a moment to consider all the things your have created in your life that that give you security and comfort.

Consider how you have put time and energy into creating financial security, stable but perhaps non-stimulating relationships, and a stable home environment.

Take a close look at your life to see how this part of you has created the different aspects of your life—how this part of you may be determining how you live.

As you connect with this part of you, spend a few moments considering how this part of you limits your life. Feel what you are missing.

Perhaps you are missing challenge, novelty, or adventure.

Perhaps you would like deeper intimacy, more love, and closeness.

Perhaps you are feeling that your life is a bit dry and stagnant, that you are not growing or living as fully as you would like to live.

Perhaps in some way, you feel that life is passing you by.

Perhaps you feel that you would like to open your heart again and feel more deeply, more intensely.

Now, imagine that you have another, very different part of you.

This is the part of you that longs for love, that knows that love is what gives life meaning.

Perhaps you can feel that this is the part of you that carries deep wisdom, the part that knows that to open your heart, you will have to take risk.

It knows that to love, to open your heart, you will have to feel more deeply, and to feel more deeply means to feel pain and hurt and insecurity and fear.

Take a few moments to experience this part of you.

Perhaps it is a part of you that has been hidden. And it may be very scary to start to connect with this part of you.

But there may also be a longing to begin to explore this unknown part and to discover what it can bring into your life.

CHAPTER 5:

WHEN ARE WE MOTIVATED
TO CHANGE?

A s you are reading this book, you may already have begun to recognize how painful it is to live in protection and have a longing for something else.

Our motivation to discover deeper layers of our being comes when:

- We recognize how stressful it is to live in the layer of protection.

- We recognize that we are living without love.

- We recognize that living in protection is not healthy for our bodies.

- We recognize that we are hurting people and hurting ourselves.

- We recognize that we have no dignity and no real power while living in protection.

For example, Steve worked for many years as a banker and managed to accumulate great wealth. He was used to living the good life, with apartments in major cities around the world, dining at the finest restaurants, and getting what he wanted from people. But as one might expect, his relationships were a disaster. He ended his affairs as soon as he felt the women were burdens to his lifestyle, or they left him in despair of his ever becoming open and available. For the past six years, he had been in an on-and-off relationship, in which they fought continually. Finally, Steve sought help because he realized that something was not working in his life.

Rachel is in love with a wealthy businessman and they have been together for five years. But she is disappointed because he is deeply absorbed in his work and is rarely present, and their communication has broken down. When we speak to her, she reveals that she has a pattern of attracting powerful, wealthy, sexy men but ends up feeling betrayed because they "don't know how to be intimate." She now recognizes that she has been seeking her Prince Charming to be the caretaker she never had, who will allow her to feel totally loved and protected.

Sometimes it takes continual disappointments, a painful rejection, the loss of a loved one, an illness, an accident, deep depression, a major financial loss, or life as we have known it seeming empty and meaningless to motivate us to change.

At this point, we face a crucial choice.

When life presents us with a painful challenge that shatters things as we have known them, we may fall into depression and resignation.

Or we may recognize this crisis as a moment of great opportunity—as a moment to change.

Instead of sinking into depression, we can reach out for help and for guidance.

This little book and CD are designed to provide that guidance for exactly such a moment in your life.

Exercise: Becoming Motivated to Change

Take a moment to consider your life.

Is it time for a change?

Has anything happened recently that has made you question the life you are living right now?

Is there something empty, frustrating, or insufficient in your connection with people?

Five years from now, if nothing has changed, would you be happy?

Most of us have reached some level of comfort in our familiar lives.

When this level of comfort becomes constrictive, empty, or no longer challenging, life is challenging us to take a step.

Now, imagine that there is a wise voice inside you.

It could be a very small voice, because you may not have listened to this voice for a long time.

Perhaps you have never tried to listen to this small voice.

But, now if you listen, you may hear this voice saying to you,

"It is time to make a change in your life."

"It is time to open your heart and let love in."

"It is time to take a risk to be vulnerable and see what that brings."

CHAPTER 6:

OPENING TO SELF-LOVE

Before opening to another, we have to open to ourselves.

Opening to ourselves means beginning to notice and feel what is happening inside.

At first that can be very frightening, as we carry many judgments about being vulnerable.

We might consider it to be weak, self-indulgent, boring, or lazy to feel and to show vulnerability.

Because of this, it is very important to bring the qualities of deep understanding and acceptance to ourselves when we are exploring these sensitive places inside.

It is with good reason that we have avoided experiencing these feelings.

It is easy to accept ourselves when we are in our essence—when we are feeling those wonderful qualities of joy, playfulness, and aliveness.

But it is much harder to love and accept our insecurity and our fear.

And it is even harder to love and accept ourselves when we are in our protection and strategies.

It may be very painful to look closely at how we have hurt the people close to us from our protection.

Practicing Self-Love—Exercise #1 Transforming Judgment to Compassion

Stand in front of a mirror.

Now open your eyes and look at yourself. Notice the judging thoughts that come into your head.

- "I am not attractive enough or sexy enough."

- "I am too old."

- "I am too fat or too skinny."

- "I am not an interesting person."

- "My body is not right."

- "My nose or ears are too big."

- "I am not alive enough."

- "I am bad."

- "I am lazy."

- "I am too selfish."

And so on.

You can even write these thoughts down if you like.

Notice how much you believe these voices.

Now close your eyes again and take three deep breaths.

Open them again.

This time, look at yourself as if you are looking through your heart.

Look at yourself with love—softly, gently, and openly.

Look especially at your eyes.

You can even imagine that the eyes in the mirror are looking at you. You are reversing the energy.

The eyes in the mirror are looking directly into you…into your heart.

Look at the whole being instead of at the small parts. These eyes can see the difficulties that you went through, and just love you.

Keep breathing deeply and notice if anything has changed from the first time.

Feel the difference.

This is looking with love.

When we are able to bring this quality of love and acceptance just a little bit more into our lives, it becomes easier to explore the fears and insecurities inside.

Practicing Self-Love—Exercise #2: Accepting Your Fears and Insecurities

Take a moment to stand in front of a mirror.

Before you open your eyes, take three deep breaths.

Now, open your eyes and look closely and deeply at your face.

Focus on seeing the fears and insecurities of this person you are looking at.

Imagine, as you explore these fears and insecurities, that this person is not you but a very close friend or even your child (if you have one).

Allow yourself to embrace this part of you and its fears and shame with your loving heart.

Realize that these feelings came from an earlier time when you were just a child and very helpless.

You could not defend yourself against invasions, intrusions, or disrespect. Or maybe things happened that were beyond anyone's control and they were frightening.

You could not understand why people were not there when you needed them or why they did not understand your needs and feelings.

You could not understand why people did not support your energy and natural gifts.

It is natural that so many fears and insecurities developed.

See if you can take this part of you into your heart.

Practicing Self-Love—Exercise #3: Accepting Your Behaviors

One of the strongest areas where we judge ourselves is for the way we behave today or have behaved in the past.

We may be harsh with ourselves for being selfish, arrogant, critical, impatient, violent, inconsiderate, or careless.

When these thoughts come up, we suggest that you ask yourself two questions:

1. *"What was my need that I was trying to fulfill that caused me to behave that way?"*

2. *"What can I learn from this and how can I grow from observing this behavior?"*

You may discover that the behavior itself was an attempt to fulfill a very important need for you. Or you may discover that the behavior is very automatic and doesn't really fulfill you any longer. Here's an example:

A woman in one of our workshops was judging herself because she said she was attracted only to men who had money. If one man disappointed her in this respect, she would move on to another man. She judged herself for being calculating, manipulative, and unkind.

We asked her,

"What need are you trying to meet with this behavior?"

She said, "As a child, we were very poor, and I needed to work hard to help support the family. My mother would beat me if I didn't bring home enough money."

"So," we answered, "it is natural that this is a strong priority for you. Perhaps later, you might discover that you are paying a price for being dependent on men in this way, and also that it is limiting your choices when your highest priority for a relationship is money. But for now, it is important to accept how much you need this financial security based on what you went through as a child. Love that little girl inside of you who is so frightened and needs financial security."

When we understand ourselves and our own stories of trauma more deeply, it is easier to have compassion for ourselves. It is easier to embrace with our hearts the behaviors that arise from our fears and insecurities.

We always have two ways to look at ourselves—either with judgment, or with compassion and understanding.

It takes a conscious decision to choose the second.

CHAPTER 7:

WHAT IS THE DIFFERENCE BETWEEN REAL VULNERABILITY AND FALSE VULNERABILITY?

There are two ways that we may experience a feeling of vulnerability.

One way is when we sense a sudden opening of our heart, most commonly when we begin a new relationship.

But it may also happen when we have a touching connection with someone or perhaps when we take a drug such as ecstasy, cocaine, or even alcohol.

Often, this feeling of openness and vulnerability may be strongest with a new lover or when we first meet a new teacher, friend, or even a therapist.

We feel stimulated, excited, inspired, loved, and perhaps deeply understood and connected.

These experiences are not what we consider "true vulnerability."

In these situations, we may be blinded by a strong sexual attraction, or the joy of finding a new friend or companion, or under the influence of a substance.

In an intimate relationship, we often begin by idealizing the other person.

We project our hopes and dreams on this person.

We also do not really see ourselves clearly in this early stage of relating.

We don't see or want to see that we are idealizing the person; we don't understand that we are projecting our own unmet needs from childhood on this person, hoping that we will get what we did not get as a child.

We all have such a hunger to be met profoundly in our energy that this hunger easily blinds us.

The feeling we have of openness, energy, and aliveness is wonderful.

And in terms of the three layers we talked about before, this is the experience of our essence layer.

What we term "true vulnerability" is different.

It is an experience of deep fear, helplessness, and insecurity that can be provoked by a financial crisis, the loss or a betrayal of a loved one, an illness, a failure, or an accident.

In these moments, our sense of security and familiarity is shaken, we may become deeply disturbed, and we may lose our trust that things will work out for the best.

It often happens when we go deeper into a relationship, our original false sense of vulnerability and openness gets replaced by a real vulnerability because we may feel that the person is not whom we believed him or her to be.

Our efforts to change the other person are frustrating failures and we must face the fears that we will not get what we hoped, that we are helpless to change the situation, and the insecurity that life will not bring us the happiness we long for

This is true vulnerability.

Let's take an example.

Richard and Cynthia fell madly in love. Both felt that they had found the partner of their dreams. Their sex life was wonderful and exciting, and after two years together, they decided to have a child. But by the time their daughter was two, they began to distance themselves from each other.

Cynthia felt Richard was sexually demanding, and jealous of the time and attention she gave to their daughter. Richard felt that Cynthia was no longer available, affectionate, or sexually interested in him. The more rejected he felt, the more critical and judgmental he became. She pulled away from him because she felt his demands and expectations, and did not feel that he was sensitive or respectful of her needs. Finally, when they came to see us, they were fighting much of the time, no longer making love, and living together as strangers.

When we explored more deeply, we discovered that Richard was frustrated in his work and felt inadequate in his profession. He was used to being pampered by his mother and expected that women would take away his pain when he was not feeling well. Because his mother treated him as her golden boy, he was also used to getting what he wanted from women and complaining when he didn't.

Cynthia's situation was quite different. Her mother had been subservient to her father, and she herself was used to obeying what her father—and later men—wanted from her. She had not learned to set limits or stand up for what she needed. But now she felt she could no longer behave as an emotional slave to a man, and was rebelling by becoming distant and cold.

We encouraged Cynthia to set her limits in a more conscious way by helping her to understand her own needs and listen to his needs without giving up her own. Unfortunately, Richard was not open to seeing how this situation was both a reflection of his unhappiness in his work and an old habit of believing that women should meet his expectations. He felt his demands were justified. After a series of couple sessions, they could see that their differences were too great and they decided to separate.

The vulnerability and openness that they both felt with each other in the beginning was false vulnerability. As soon as one person was no longer as the other person wanted him or her to be, they closed.

They were not able or willing to take the next step of exposing their true vulnerability to each other. They no longer had enough trust.

Richard was not willing to go deeper and connect with his true vulnerability because he felt justified in his demands and wanted to be right. To let go of his demands and his need to be right would mean that he would have to feel and admit his insecurity and shame about not feeling successful in the world. He would also have to feel his fears of not getting his basic emotional and sexual needs met. That would be his true vulnerability.

Cynthia was more willing to explore her deep fears of confronting men and being honest instead of expressing her anger indirectly by pulling away and feeling resentful. But she would have to learn this lesson in her next relationship.

It takes great courage to feel true vulnerability.

True vulnerability comes when we are willing to recognize, admit, and feel our pain, fear, and insecurity when we are helpless to change things outside of us.

It comes when we are ready to not hide behind masks.

It is a vulnerability that comes when we no longer blame other people or the world for our unhappiness and unmet expectations.

True vulnerability comes when we feel the pain we experience in our lives today when someone or something disappoints us.

And instead of moving automatically into anger, disappointment, resignation, or blame, we see how this situation triggers unmet basic needs from our past and feel the pain of the earlier times when we felt hurt, disappointed, and disrespected.

Opening our true vulnerability involves five important aspects:

1. We are willing to see that the *disappointments that get triggered today are rooted in our past.*

2. We are willing to see *how our past still runs our life today in our reactions.*

3. We are willing to *feel the pain, fear, insecurity, and shock* that we still hold inside because of how we were treated in the past.

4. We are willing to investigate our *expectations* and *patterns of behavior* that push people away.

5. We are willing to *learn new ways of relating* to people and life that are not based on our past.

Exercise: Noticing the difference between true and false vulnerability

Take a moment to observe your most significant relationships.

- In what ways have you felt disappointed or even betrayed?

- In what ways has this person changed from when you first met him or her?

- What expectations have not been or are not being met?

- What would you have to feel if you stopped trying to change that person?

The vulnerability you felt before you had to encounter disappointment was what we call "false vulnerability."

The vulnerability you have to face when you encounter disappointment is what we call "true vulnerability."

CHAPTER 8:

HOW CAN WE LEARN TO OPEN OUR REAL VULNERABILITY?

*T*he following guided meditations and exercises are designed to provide you with simple and concrete tools for bringing a deeper sense of vulnerability into your life.

A Simple Heart Meditation

Take a moment to focus your attention to the area of your heart and chest.

When we say *heart*, we are talking about the energetic heart that is the whole area of your upper body, from shoulder to shoulder and down to the solar plexus.

This is where we carry our true vulnerability.

Take a few moments just to breathe into this area, bringing all your focus and concentration to the sensation in this area.

What do you feel?

Is it tight?

Is it sore and aching?

Is it a bit numb?

This is the place where we carry all the hurts and fears we have gathered in our lives.

This is the area where we absorbed rejections and abuse—from ex-lovers or current lovers, from our friends, from other students in school, from our parents

Perhaps there is a heaviness in this area.

Perhaps there is sadness.

Let your heart talk to you.

Maybe it is just a tremble.

Or maybe it is saying, "I am so sad."

Or, "I don't want to open again."

Or just, "Why?"

"Why are people so insensitive?"

"Why don't people really listen to me or understand me?"

Your heart is no longer the innocent and trusting heart of a young child.

Now it is a wounded heart of an adult who has been traumatized.

Listening to your wounded heart is the best way to feel your true vulnerability.

A Meditation on Your Childhood

Now, let's go a step deeper.

Imagine that you are a young boy or girl, perhaps six years old.

See yourself back in the house where you lived when you were around that age.

Look around and notice who is in your home at this time.

Perhaps it is evening time and you notice your mother and your father or another caretaker at home.

If one of them is absent, notice and feel that.

- How does it feel in this home?

- How is it to be a child in this home?

- Are your mother and father happy together?

- Most of the time, are they fighting or loving each other?

- Do you feel safe in this house?

- Do you feel loved?

- Do you feel that you are seen as unique and precious?

- Do you feel safe and protected?

- If not, what is happening that is making you feel unsafe?

- How does it feel in your body not to feel safe?

- Are you feeling judged or pressured or criticized by anyone?

- In general, what is difficult for you?

- What do you need that you are not getting?

Opening to Your Vulnerability in Your Daily Life

These simple but profound questions are a way to opening your vulnerability again.

In our everyday lives, we are given many opportunities that provoke our vulnerability.

Every hurt, insensitivity, or loveless act that we received in our lives is remembered in our hearts.

And when we were small children, we did not yet have armor to protect ourselves against other people being insensitive to us.

Slowly over time we have built an armor that now is non-discriminating. It is constantly there. Even when it is safe to open again at times in our lives, we are protected.

The way to begin to open your vulnerability again is to become sensitive to your heart and to feel how incredibly sensitive you were as a young child.

When you begin to feel this sensitivity, you also begin to feel the effect that other people had on you when you were small.

And you will begin to feel that you are just as sensitive today when you feel hurt, rejected, invaded, not listened to, or when you feel humiliated by someone.

An Exercise For When You Feel Hurt or Disturbed— "The Inner Process"

There may be times when you don't receive the approval and attention that you would like from someone. Perhaps it is a lover, a friend, a sibling, or an authority figure.

Sometimes someone says something rude to you, and you are in such shock that you can't say anything back.

Sometimes you feel hurt because you are not feeling as loved by someone as you would like.

These are moments that happen to all of us, but often we don't take the time to feel what is happening inside.

Normally when we are disturbed, we don't take the time to stop and feel the disturbance. We usually move directly into a reaction.

Perhaps we get angry, we give up, or we try to change the other person or the situation. Perhaps we apologize and feel guilty, or perhaps we try to fix things. Or we may pretend that it doesn't matter.

All of these reactions can be very automatic and compulsive.

They happen very fast.

We move immediately from disturbance into reaction.

Now as we bring awareness to this situation, we are suggesting instead to stop and feel.

We call this *"The Inner Process."*

Even if you already have reacted, once you realize you have reacted, you can stop and feel.

Ask yourself, *"What am I feeling right now?"* and then feel the sensations in your body.

Ask yourself, *"What is the fear right now?"* and then feel the sensations of fear in your body.

What does your body tell you?

Perhaps you are very *tense and anxious.*

Perhaps you feel very *heavy and guilty.*

Perhaps you feel *angry.*

Perhaps you feel a sense of collapse and low energy.

Ask yourself, *"What would I have needed in this situation that I didn't receive? What would I have needed to feel loved?"*

Ask yourself, *"How is this situation a reminder of something from my past?"*

Taking the time to stop and ask yourself these questions opens you to your vulnerability.

Situations that Provoke our Vulnerability

There are a number of situations in our lives today that can bring up our vulnerability.

- When we have to perform something or take a risk to express ourselves in a new way.

- When we are in the presence of an authority figure or someone else we respect, and we would like his or her attention and approval.

- When someone says or does something disrespectful to us.

- When someone rejects us or when we suffer a loss of someone important.

- When someone is not loving us the way we would like.

- When we are sick or are involved in an accident.

- When we lose a job or experience a failure at work.

- When we are attracted to someone and feel very insecure.

In these situations, it is good to ask yourself, "What is my fear and insecurity?"

Then take time to feel the sensations in the body.

CHAPTER 9:

HOW CAN WE OPEN OUR VULNERABILITY TO SOMEONE ELSE?

I t is not easy to feel vulnerable, for all the reasons we have mentioned before.

We don't want to feel these uncomfortable feelings.

We would rather run away into some kind of reaction, distraction, or addiction.

But it is even more challenging to feel vulnerable with another person.

It can be very frightening to show our fears and insecurities, and to even admit them to another person.

Many of us have been taught that it is not good to show our fears or insecurities, and that it is better to pretend we are fine.

Most of us have been taught that vulnerability is weakness, and believe that if we show our weaknesses, people will not respect us or they will take advantage of us.

The problem with living with this belief is that if we don't feel or expose our insecurities and fears, we will stay locked in a lonely cave, shut out from love and true connection.

We can also become hard, depressed, bitter, and deeply unhappy.

A big part of coming home again to life, to love, and to ourselves involves sharing our vulnerability with other people.

Of course, it is not appropriate to show this vulnerability to everyone. It has to be someone with whom we feel some safety.

A good place to practice showing vulnerability is with a friend that you love and feel safe with.

An Exercise with a Friend

The next time you are with a good friend, share what it is about him or her that you like and how it feels for you to be friends.

Share what you feel with this friend that you don't feel with other people.

What is it about this friend and your friendship that allows you to feel these deeper feelings?

Talk about what it would be like to share with this friend if you had a difficult time such as a rejection, loss, accident, illness, or disrespect from someone.

Share what it would be like to ask for support if you were about to start something new and were insecure about it.

As you read this exercise, you may even be able to feel in your heart what it feels like to have a good friend with whom you can talk about anything, even difficult feelings.

You may be missing such a friend in your life.

An Exercise with a Lover

This time, we suggest an exercise that is a bit more challenging.

Sit in front of your lover. If you are not in a love relationship at present, you can pick someone to represent a future lover.

It is important that this is a time when you are not feeling provoked, angry, or disconnected from him or her.

You can say to your partner, "I would like to share some sensitive feelings about myself and I wonder if you would like to listen. This has nothing to do with you; it is just a part of me that I would like to share with you so that you can know me better."

Allow yourself to feel the part of you inside that holds your fears and insecurities—the wounded child.

Begin to share something about yourself that you are ashamed of or still judge about yourself.

Also, share with this person any fears and insecurities you feel about coming close to people, about succeeding in life, about making money, about your creativity, about growing old, about relationships with your parents—in short, any topic where you might have some fear or insecurity.

Share your fears of opening to this person in particular.

Share your insecurities that perhaps you are not enough, not a good enough lover, or anything else in which you might feel deficient and inadequate.

Share your fears of rejection, or fears that he or she might leave you for someone else.

Share your fears of losing yourself, of not being able to feel yourself if you open more deeply.

Share your fears of losing your freedom.

How does it feel when you share these sensitive feelings?

Do you feel more open and connected to your partner?

Do you feel more open and connected to yourself?

Exercise: Sharing When You Feel Disturbed with a Person

This is the most challenging situation for being vulnerable with someone.

(For this exercise, we would like to give credit to the work of Marshal Rosenberg called Non-violent Communication, whose training we did some years ago.)

It is difficult to be vulnerable when you feel angry, hurt, or distant from someone.

It is more customary to want to pull away, attack, analyze, punish, try to change, or make demands on the person who we are disturbed with.

When we feel hurt by someone, we go rapidly and automatically into our protection, and often we want to hurt that person for hurting us.

In this exercise, we guide you to reconnect and repair by sharing your vulnerability.

When you feel hurt, attacked, rejected, ignored, or judged by someone, it causes hurt.

Often, there is something that we would like to say and perhaps need to say to that person.

If we don't say anything, we most likely will cut ourselves off from that person. If it is someone close, such as a close friend or a lover, it will eventually destroy the relationship.

When we don't clear up a hurt, we build resentment and distance.

Perhaps we do say something, but it comes out in anger, as an attack, judgment, punishment, or analysis of the other. That way of responding creates more hurt and distance.

The first step when you feel hurt is to go in, as we guided you in the last chapter—to go through *"The Inner Process."*

Explore the feelings of hurt, the fears, and the basic needs that were not met in that situation.

Also ask yourself how this situation reminds you of your past, especially your childhood.

When you feel that you are centered and no longer strongly emotional, that is the time to practice this exercise.

It only works when you no longer have the desire to change, fix, attack, analyze, blame, accuse, or criticize the other person.

It only works when you sincerely have a desire to make a connection.

When this is the case, you can come to the other person.

Here we give you some clear steps to help you have a structure for this exercise:

1. Ask the person:

"I would like to share something with you that is important for me and for our connection. Would you have the space right now to listen while I share?"

"This is about me. I would like to share as a way of telling you more about myself and also so that our connection becomes better. I commit not to blame, attack, analyze, criticize, or to try to change you. I would like to take ten minutes to share and would ask you to listen without interrupting me. Then if you like, I would like to give the same time to you and I promise to listen without interrupting you."

If the person says yes, then you can continue. If they say no, then all you can do at this time is wait and feel the disappointment that may be there. You can ask the other person to let you know when they feel ready to listen and connect.

2. If he or she says "yes," then follow these steps:

The first sentence in your sharing is, "When you did or said ..., I felt ... ."

(When you describe what he or she did that upset you, just relate the simple facts of what happened, without any interpretation or analysis. Just the facts! When you describe the feeling, use few and simple words such as, "I felt hurt, sad, or angry, or misunderstood, ignored, or abandoned.)

3. Then go on to taking it back to your past.

"When this happened, it reminded me of an earlier time (when I was a child, when I was with an ex-lover, etc.) when a similar thing happened to me and I felt...."

4. Share the basic need that was not met for you in this situation, and how it was similar to the basic need that was not met when you were a child. Share your feelings about this deep wound in you that was provoked in this situation.

5. "I wonder how you feel about my sharing this. Would you like to say something?"

In this exercise, if you are vulnerable, you probably will feel closer to the person afterwards and he or she will most likely also feel closer to you.

But if you attacked, blamed, judged, analyzed, or tried to change this person, there may be more distance and hostility.

It is a good thing to remember that vulnerability brings more love, and protection brings more distance.

And of course, if you want more love in your life, you have to be the one to initiate being vulnerable and open. That is a big risk.

If you wait for the other person to open in order to feel safe to open, that is just another power game, another form of protection.

CHAPTER 10:

HOW TO BE VULNERABLE TO LIFE

The greatest step in opening to our vulnerability again is becoming vulnerable to life itself.

There is an old Chinese story of an old man who owned a very beautiful horse. The horse was envied by the king, who offered him a fabulous price to buy it from him, but the man refused.

"This horse is my friend, my best friend, so I cannot sell him," he said.

All the villagers thought he was crazy to turn down such an offer, especially since some time afterwards, the horse ran away.

The villagers said to him, "What a horrible thing has happened. Now you don't have the horse, and you are poor when you could have been rich. What a terrible misfortune!"

The old man said, "I wouldn't say that. I would only say that the horse is gone."

Some time later, the horse returned, bringing with him a dozen other beautiful wild horses.

Now the villagers said, "What good fortune you have had! You are truly blessed!"

The old man said, "I wouldn't go that far. I would only say that the horse is back. Who knows what will come?"

One day, his only son fell from the horse and broke both his legs and became crippled.

The villagers said, "What a terrible misfortune. Your son can no longer work and will not be able to support you."

Again, the old man responded, "Don't go that far; you never know. All I can say is that my son has broken his legs."

Some weeks later, the country went to war and all the young men of the town were drafted. Most died in battle and never returned.

The people came to the old man and said, "You are the luckiest man in the town because your son was spared. What a blessing!"

The old man said, "One can never jump to conclusions. Only God sees the whole picture."

We often judge because we do not understand.

Most of us are not as surrendered to or as trusting of life as this old man.

But learning to be vulnerable to life means learning to accept what happens in our lives that we have no control over.

It is easy to be open to life when it is going our way, when things are happening the way we would like them to happen.

It is easy when we feel loved, but not so easy when we feel rejected or ignored.

It is easy when our creativity is being rewarded and we are successful. It is not so easy when we experience failure or financial difficulties.

It is easy to be open to life when our health is good, our energy is high, and we feel positive.

It is not so easy to stay open when we are sick, when we feel discouraged, and when we have negative thoughts.

Perhaps we have some idea that it is important to be positive and accepting of everything.

Perhaps we have some idea that we should take every experience as a learning experience and never become negative.

Perhaps we have learned that we should never complain about anything.

All these teachings may be right, but if they are only ideas, they have little value for taking us to true vulnerability with life.

When things are difficult and not going our way, most of the time we cannot simply put smiles on our faces.

If we suffer a painful rejection, if we are not getting the love we need in a relationship, if we have suffered a painful loss, if we experience failure and we feel deeply discouraged, it does not work to pretend that everything is fine.

In that moment, everything does not feel fine. It feels painful.

To open to our vulnerability in these difficult moments, we have to allow ourselves first to feel the feelings that come up.

If we feel pain and hurt, we have to feel that pain and hurt in our hearts.

If we feel angry, we have to feel that anger in our bodies and perhaps go into the forest and express it—or beat a pillow, or dance an angry dance.

If we feel discouraged and without motivation, it is important to allow those feelings and feel them.

If we are afraid of doing something and notice that we are postponing it, it is good to feel the fear and accept it.

Becoming vulnerable to life means being willing to accept whatever state we find ourselves in with compassion.

Any idea of how we should be or how we should act is not helpful. In fact, it interferes with true vulnerability.

The moments where life is treating us kindly, we can feel those and be grateful.

The moments where life is presenting us with difficult challenges, we are invited to feel those as well

We may not feel grateful in those moments.

We might even feel very angry with someone, with life, or with God or existence for putting us in a particular situation.

Perhaps it will take time to discover what we have learned from this challenging situation. It may take a lot of time before we are able to see and feel how we have changed inside and before we feel grateful for what happened.

Vulnerability to life means saying "yes" to life.

It means saying "yes" to whatever comes, even if it is very painful.

It means opening the heart to everything.

It means accepting the fact that often we are helpless.

We cannot change how our parents are or how they treated us when we were young.

We cannot change our lover or close friend.

And the moments when we don't receive from them what we would like may be painful.

Saying "yes" to life also means saying "yes" to our limitations.

It may be hard sometimes to accept that in some respects and in some areas, we are not what we would like to be.

Perhaps we are not as attractive, as young, as intelligent, as charismatic, as rich, or as wise as someone we compare ourselves with.

Many of us may have fantasies that our lives will go on forever.

Ultimately, becoming vulnerable to life means accepting that at some point, we will have to let go of everything we have known and become attached to.

CONCLUSION:

THE GIFT OF VULNERABILITY

We have mentioned that opening our vulnerability is the way to coming back home to ourselves again and to love. Why is this so?

What is the gift of opening our vulnerability?

Many of us have been taught that vulnerability is weakness.

Actually, the opposite is true.

Vulnerability is our greatest power.

When we open to our vulnerability, we gain tremendous self-respect.

When we allow ourselves to feel the fears and shame inside, we become human beings.

We become trustworthy.

This is the way we become loving and lovable.

It is the way that our heart opens.

Pain is the greatest teacher in life, and there is no other way to open the heart.

Those who have not felt their pain, those who judge their fears and cannot accept their insecurities and shame, become hard inside and can even become cruel.

When we don't accept our vulnerability, we are hard on ourselves and then we are usually equally hard on others.

What we avoid feeling in ourselves, we don't want to feel in others because it reminds us unconsciously of what we are repressing.

So we judge and condemn it.

It is the same with pain, fear, and insecurity as it is with aliveness, joy, passion, and courage.

It is all energy.

If we repress parts of our energy we also have less aliveness.

Opening to our vulnerability is the way home to becoming whole.

It is the way of inviting love into our lives.

In our protected shells, we see the world as a place where we must hide and defend.

Yes, we have to use our intelligence and learn to discriminate with whom and how we open.

And in our opening, there are no guarantees that things will work out the way we would like them to.

For sure, there will be pain and disappointments.

And through that we will grow and become wiser, more mature human beings.

It brings a richness into our lives that staying in our protection can never bring.

It brings color into our lives.

It is like learning to live and explore all the colors of the rainbow.

PART 2

LETTING GO –

Recovering from Rejection and Abandonment

TABLE OF CONTENTS

INTRODUCTION:

RELATING IS ONE OF LIFE'S GREATEST CHALLENGES

Peter came to see Krish because his girlfriend had just left him for another man. He was devastated. He had never been to see a therapist before but at this time, he didn't know how to deal with the pain he was feeling and he needed help. He needed to understand how she could just reject him so suddenly. She was the love of his life and although they had problems, he thought they could solve them together. But now she was gone, spending time and making love with another man. The thought was driving him crazy. He wanted to know what he had done wrong. He wanted to know how he could get her back!

Suzanne also came to us because her boyfriend, Martin, said that he no longer wanted to be in a monogamous relationship. She had done many workshops in the past and she felt she was finished with therapy. She was furious with him and felt he was simply avoiding his fears. As far as she was concerned, it was him that needed to be in therapy. She wanted us to convince him that he needed to work on himself and teach him to face his fears of intimacy. As far as she was concerned, she had nothing to explore in herself even though she had a long history of being with men who had left her for one reason or another.

When the experience of rejection hits us, there are many ways we can deal with it, but it always hurts.

- Perhaps we blame the other person, or blame ourselves.

- Perhaps we sink into depression and give up on love and relationships.

- Perhaps we drive ourselves crazy trying to figure out what we did wrong or how we could have behaved differently.

- Perhaps we feel so unworthy that we become convinced that no one can ever love us again.

- Perhaps we try to lose ourselves in work or activities, or we turn to alcohol or drugs to avoid feeling the pain.

This part of the book and the CD of the same title is designed to help you deal with situations of rejection or loss.

These moments are great tests in our lives.

We can either go in the direction of blame, anger, depression, hopelessness, and bitterness, or we can grow and learn from these situations.

These are the moments when the greatest inner growth is possible because we grow with pain when there is understanding and awareness.

Pain takes us out of our normal, structured, armored, secure lives and gives us a jolt of awakening.

It cracks us open and we become vulnerable.

Even in the best love stories, we will never get everything we hope for. Life is very fragile and unpredictable.

We never know how long the love or time together will last.

We are faced with a choice.

We can choose to shut our windows and doors and not let love in, or we can chose to open to love and intimacy, knowing that it will bring pain.

We can learn how to stay present with the pain and grow from it when it comes.

This book will help you learn how.

CHAPTER 1:

WHY IS REJECTION SO PAINFUL?

L et's begin by bringing some *understanding* as to why rejection happens and what it brings up for us.

Why is it so disturbing when someone rejects us or when we lose someone we love?

For two reasons:

The first reason is that it brings up deep feelings of unworthiness that have been buried inside, which most of us have not wanted to look at.

This is the wound of *shame.*

This is a space of feeling profoundly insufficient, deficient, and inadequate, and that we are fundamentally wrong.

The second reason is that it opens another wound that is also hidden in our unconscious.

This is the wound of *abandonment.*

This wound is a deep experience of feeling unwanted, lonely, neglected, and uncared for.

Both have their origins in comparison, neglect, lack of support, insensitivity, and lack of emotional attunement in childhood.

When it is provoked in our lives today, it is often surprisingly painful.

When Peter came to see Krish to work with the pain of his rejection, he had been together with his ex-girlfriend for a year and had enjoyed a wonderful wild time exploring life, sexuality, and tender moments together. It was the first time in many years that he had been in a relationship. The last two months before their breakup, things had not been going well. She pressured him to get married and live together, and he felt that it was too fast for him. She also began having bouts of heavy drinking that disturbed him. He also began to notice that she was focused mostly on her own needs and was insensitive to his.

He felt deeply betrayed.

All his old mistrust of women came up.

"I gave her everything I could. I took care of her. I went out of my way to please her. I even gave up my one day off in the week to go shopping with her. It meant that we had to travel one hour each way from where I was working because she didn't want to go alone.

"And about this marriage thing, I just wasn't ready. It was too fast for me. But she couldn't hear it. I think that she was just thinking of herself all the time."

At the same time, he was not only devastated that she no longer wanted to be with him, but he also started doubting himself as a man. He felt inadequate as a lover and judged himself heavily because he could not give her what she wanted. He felt that he should have been ready to marry her and he should have been more selfless.

In his opinion, his own needs were not important because "if I really love a woman, I should be able to love her unconditionally."

He felt confused, angry, hurt, and profoundly anxious. He could not understand why he was feeling so badly and could not find a way to deal with all his feelings.

He told Krish that now he was drinking heavily at night "just to relax and be able to sleep."

Even though rationally he knew that the relationship probably was not going to work, it did nothing to calm his pain and anxiety.

He obsessed about talking to her, dreamed about her, ruminated about their good times together, and deeply missed the physical connection they had.

When he came to see Krish, he did not know how he could ever recover from this loss.

The experience of abandonment and rejection is not rational.

Often it makes no sense at all why we are feeling so much pain.

The pain that we feel seems so much more intense than what we would expect.

And often when the abandonment wounds get triggered, we are so disturbed that we cannot function in our regular lives.

The rejection, loss, or abandonment in our lives today are triggers for much older and deeper wounds.

When we experience rejection in our lives today, the hidden wounds of childhood abuse or neglect surface like an emotional tsunami overwhelming our conscious mind.

As a child, Peter was regularly beaten and humiliated by his father, and his mother was too afraid of his father to defend him. Until Krish discussed these early experiences with him, he never suspected that there was anything wrong with how his father treated him, or that his mother could not protect him. He just thought that he was not good enough as a son to win his father's approval. He also never realized how much fear he still held inside because of his father's abuse.

Maria had been seeing Amana regularly in individual therapy for several years. She felt continually devastated because her lover of seven years, Leonard, was not willing to commit to marriage. As a result, she felt deeply insecure, unloved, and unappreciated and she continually complained or raged at him. She was confused because when they were together, they actually had wonderful times. Their lovemaking was sensitive, both gentle and explosive, and nourishing. They enjoyed the same things in life and shared each other's love for art, gourmet food, and beautiful places. But whenever she brought up the topic of marriage and commitment, they would fight and she would end up feeling rejected.

Krish and Amana worked intensively with both of them individually and in couple's sessions. Each had profound experiences of neglect, disrespect, and lack of support as children. Each felt deep mistrust of the opposite sex.

Maria easily lost herself whenever she came close to a strong man, and it brought her back to childhood moments when her father was overly seductive and possessive and her mother cold and distant. She would give up her work and her friends and be ready to be with Leonard whenever he wanted. She would then become resentful whenever he needed some time alone.

Leonard felt that the slightest demand from a woman reminded him of his overbearing and aggressive mother. Over time, they learned to separate their childhood experiences from those of today. They worked intensively with feeling the pain of these early childhood traumas and understanding how profoundly they affected their fears and reactive behavior today in their relationship.

They each learned to set appropriate limits on their time and needs. They each learned to communicate their hurts, anxieties, and mistrust without blaming or reacting to the other. They are slowly building trust between them, becoming able to listen to and feel the other person without feeling threatened by the other person's emotional experience. They no longer feel the other as a threat or as a source of frustration of their basic needs.

Peter's journey of healing his abandonment wound was also impressive. He came to realize how his compulsive pleasing behavior and denial of his own needs came from the shock and trauma of his father's treatment, and to feel the profound effect this had on his fears and insecurity as a man. As the work progressed, he came to appreciate his own gentleness and sensitivity as well as his strength. He learned that he could be loved even if he respected and stood up for his own needs, and to say "no" when he was asked to do something that did not feel right to him.

And most importantly, he learned that he is not his father—that when he does come into his strength, he does not become his abusive father. He stopped drinking excessively and would allow himself alcohol only occasionally when he would party with friends, and then just in moderation. Six months into his work with Krish, he received an unexpected call from his ex-partner asking to see him. When they got together, they both realized that there was still much love between them and they tentatively began seeing each other again. This time it was different as he was now able to set firm limits, and he told her that their ongoing commitment to each other was dependent on her also seeking counseling.

CHAPTER 2:

WHAT ARE THESE PAST ABANDONMENT EXPERIENCES?

When we get rejected or lose someone close to us, what is it exactly that gets triggered from our past?

Here are some of the hidden feelings and memories that might get awakened:

1. We didn't feel welcomed or received as a child.

2. A parent died or became physically or mentally ill when we were young.

3. We felt neglected in the ways we were being cared for and loved.

4. We were not given the feeling that we are special and unique.

5. We were abused physically.

6. We were abused sexually.

7. We experienced being controlled, possessed, or emotionally manipulated by one or both of our parents.

8. We were humiliated, criticized, pressured, or judged at home or at school.

9. One or both of our parents were alcoholics or substance abusers.

10. One or both of our parents were depressed, sickly, repressive, or chronically negative about life.

11. One or both of our parents left the family.

12. We were raised in a community and lacked the personal attention of one or both parents.

13. Our parents divorced.

14. One of our parents carried on a secret affair.

15. Our parents were often actively or silently fighting.

16. We were conditioned to play a role in the family instead of being supported to be ourselves.

17. We had to physically and/or emotionally take care of one or both of our parents or our siblings.

18. We carried the expectations of one or both of our parents to succeed or become something or someone.

19. We had to take too much responsibility too early and didn't have time to play and be a child.

20. We were not given limits, or we lacked structure, or we were not taught to care for our body, our feelings, and our personal space.

21. We were not taught how to listen to our intuition.

This is quite a list, isn't it?

So it is little wonder that all of us carry abandonment memories in our unconscious just waiting to be triggered.

Why does it need a trigger to open up the wound?

When we are young and are exposed to any one of the experiences on the list above, we do not feel that we are being abandoned.

We feel that this is just how life is.

We seldom feel the pain; we come to accept that this is normal.

Children grasp at whatever positive experiences they receive and idealize their parents, teachers, or authority figures.

As children, we have to idealize them because they are all we have.

And even today, if someone suggests something negative about these people from our past, we often defend them.

Rather than face the traumas we experienced, we often choose to deny or minimize that anything damaging or painful happened to us.

Or we may simply say, "He (or she) also had a difficult childhood and didn't really mean to hurt me. They did the best they could."

We are not aware how deeply these traumas affect our lives and abilities to relate today.

A child who is mistreated, neglected, or abandoned comes to believe that he or she deserves to be treated this way.

And then he or she comes to expect this kind of treatment.

Here's the way all this shows itself in our lives today.

We are living our lives, unaware of the way we have been damaged or how past traumatic experiences influence our daily lives.

Then we experience a rejection or loss.

The emotional tsunami comes ... and the pain seems overwhelming.

The intensity of the pain, fear, and disturbance takes us totally by surprise and we have no idea how to deal with it.

We may become self-destructive, or we may strike out at the person who hurt us, or we may strike out at people or life in general because we are hurting so much inside.

We may get lost in some kind of addictive behavior to numb the pain.

We may sink into deep depression and lose our energy and motivation to function in life.

Because these experiences can be so overwhelming, it is important to understand what is happening and to reach out for help.

The *first step in the healing and recovery process* is being helped to understand that the experience of today is just the tip of the iceberg. We are helped to make the connection between present and past, connecting the trigger to the source.

There is no doubt that a rejection, loss, or abandonment in our life today can be terribly painful.

But if it were not for the fact that it is opening up buried pain from the past, we could recover and move on with our lives much more quickly.

We would not be so hard on ourselves when painful events happen, and therefore be more ready to actually feel the pain.

What is causing most of our pain is the *buried pain from the past*—the pain of abandonment and traumatic experiences that we experienced when we were far too young to be able to understand, process, make any kind of sense of, or feel what was happening to us.

The event today is an opportunity to feel what we could not feel as a child.

Exercise: *Connecting past and present hurts*

Take a moment to consider a recent or less recent experience of rejection.

Ask yourself:

- What feelings did this experience provoke?

- In what ways did you feel inadequate?

- In what ways did you feel that you did something wrong?

- In what ways did you feel betrayed?

- Did you feel similar feelings in your past, specifically in your childhood?

CHAPTER 3:

WHAT SHOULD WE ASK OURSELVES WHEN WE GET REJECTED?

When we get rejected, we usually obsess about the same questions over and over.

"How did this happen?"

"Why did it happen?"

"What did I do wrong?"

"Why could she not understand how much I loved her?"

"If only I had done this or said that, he would never have left me."

"Maybe if I call and explain, things will change and she will take me back."

"I know that I can convince him that I have changed and that things will be different from now on."

You might even want to give the person who rejected you a gift to prove that you are a loving, thoughtful person, or find some way to see him or her.

You go to your friends and ask them, "What should I do? Do you think that if I do that, it will make a difference? What do you think she needs to make her love me again?"

We want someone to talk to, a shoulder to lean on, someone who will listen.

We want to share our pain, perhaps with a friend or even a parent.

Perhaps we want to complain about how we were treated.

Or we want some advice about what we can do to get the other person back.

We might want to talk about how terrible we feel about ourselves.

Or we want someone to agree with us that the other person treated us badly and disrespectfully.

Friends can easily get tired of hearing the same stories and the same obsessive thoughts over and over again.

All of these thoughts and questions are natural.

But the most important question is:

"How can I prevent this from happening again?"

I (Krish) remember clearly that the last time I experienced a rejection I knew that I needed more than just a friend to talk to. I needed someone who could ask me deeper questions, someone who was trained to guide me to learn from the experience and grow from it.

It is not telling our story that heals us.

It is what we learn from telling our story that sets us on the path of recovery.

Here are some deeper questions to ask yourself:

How did you feel about yourself in this relationship? Did you feel as an equal, inferior, or superior?

Did you slip into a role or roles in this relationship—as caretaker, provider, mother, father, child, teacher, student, guru, or disciple?

In what way did you lose yourself in this relationship?

In what ways were you not able to stand up for yourself in this relationship?

In what ways did your fears of being rejected affect the relationship?

These questions are appropriate for any significant relationship in your life.

I (Krish) went to see a therapist and she helped me to see how I was still repeating old patterns that came from my childhood. I was still so insecure at that stage in my life that I attracted women who needed me to rescue them. I was too afraid to be with someone who was my equal, because I was afraid that then I would be rejected.

Each of us has a different story and different ways we repeat old patterns today.

But some things we all have in common.

- We all learned roles from our childhood to make us feel worthy of love. Then we play these roles in our relationships today to prove to ourselves and to the other person that we are worthy of love. There is deep shame and insecurity associated with the feeling that we are not good enough—not lovable, successful, sensitive, attractive, alive, intelligent, dynamic, or creative enough—and we bring all that unworthiness into our relationship today.

- There is also deep hunger for love, and anxiety that we will never get the love, attention, approval, recognition, or caring that we need.

- We carry the expectation of being rejected—a fear that something bad and harmful will happen to us and that things are not going to work out for the best.

- We are so afraid of being rejected because of our past that in our relationships today, we avoid really opening by hiding in expectations, power games, and strategies of control or manipulation.

To heal from abandonment experiences, we need to see our lives as continuous processes of events that have shaped us.

These events have built inside of us, forming our beliefs, feelings, and behaviors toward ourselves, others, and life itself.

With patience and with someone listening skillfully, carefully and compassionately, gently guiding us with support and validation, we begin to see how the events of today are so powerfully affected by our past.

We begin to see the connection.

We begin to understand how rejection is already built in to the way we are approaching our relationships.

For instance, here are some possibilities of what we might discover:

- I get rejected because when I come close to someone, I lose myself and I lose my power. I lose myself because I am so deeply insecure.

- I get rejected because when I allow someone to come close to me, I pull away and make it difficult or impossible for him or her to reach me. I do this because I am so afraid of being hurt.

- I get rejected because I don't feel that I am attractive or loveable.

- I get rejected because I feel that I am worthless and a failure, and I cannot understand how anyone can respect me since I don't even respect myself.

- My relationships fail because I cover my insecurities with my need to be in control. I need to be in control because I am afraid that if I allow myself to be vulnerable, I will be hurt or rejected.

- I get rejected because I am ashamed about my sexuality. So after a while being with someone, I cut off and stop wanting sex.

- I get rejected because I am so needy and demanding. I am like this because I am afraid that I will never get the love or attention that I need.

- My relationships fail because I am overly focused on myself. I have always been like this because I have been afraid that if I weren't focused on myself, I would never get the respect and success I want.

- I get rejected because I make my partner dependent on me. I am more comfortable being needed than being needy, but then the other person gets resentful that I have the power and am not vulnerable.

- I get rejected because I become emotionally dependent on my partner. I am afraid of being alone, but then my partner resents my being so dependent.

Exercise: Your Childhood Abandonment Experiences

Take a few moments to relax.

Take a few deep breaths.

Imagine that with the awareness you have today, you are going back to your childhood home to explore what it what like for you as a child.

You closely observe your surroundings and you notice all the people who are there, including yourself as a child of about seven years old.

Imagine that you are standing next to yourself as a child, and you are now able to feel him or her as if it were you. And since you are now much older, it is easier to feel things because you have some distance.

What does it feel like for this child to be in this household?

Does this child feel safe, special, received, and felt?

Are the child's parents present, concerned, and involved with him or her?

Are they taking time to listen to him or her?

If not, how are they with each other and how does that feel to this child?

How does this child feel about himself or herself?

Is this child confident, energetic, joyful, happy, and playful?

If not, why not?

How do this child's parents and the environment support his or her aliveness?

Is this child supported in exploring, creating, and discovering himself or herself?

Is there time for this child? Or does this child get forgotten among all the other children?

Is this child asked to play a role in this family from an early age?

These are all quite deep questions helping you to explore your early abandonment experiences.

Take time to consider them.

CHAPTER 4:

BIG AND LITTLE REJECTIONS

There are two kinds of rejections.

The first is when someone leaves us or dies.

We call these *the big rejections.*

Most of us have experienced this kind of rejection at some time in our lives, or are still experiencing it in this moment.

We never forget these experiences, and when we recover, we may sincerely hope that they never happen again.

There is another kind of rejection or abandonment that is not so easy to recognize, but very important to deal with.

These are the rejections you feel when someone you are close to is not giving you the love and attention you would like.

These are the rejections you feel when someone close to you is not the way you would like him or her to be, or is behaving in a way you don't approve of.

These are the rejections you feel when someone turns out to be different from what you thought he or she was in the beginning of the relationship.

This is the pain you feel when he or she pulls away from you, criticizes you, doesn't support you, is not present enough, or ignores you.

We call these *the little rejections or abandonments*.

We call them "little"—not because they feel little, because they don't.

They feel like huge betrayals, and they can easily make us feel enormous frustration and helplessness.

We call them "little" because in any relationship of any significance, they happen all the time in little ways.

For instance:

- You feel it when your partner is spending too much time on the computer or does not share enough with you.

- You feel it when your partner is not able to express his or her feelings, doesn't want to share feelings, or perhaps is not connected to his or her feelings.

- You feel it when your partner is too busy or not present for any reason.

- You feel it when you don't like your partner's smell, when he or she neglects his or her body, or when he or she is depressed or spends too much time watching television.

- You feel it when your partner drinks or smokes too much.

- You feel it when your partner does not want sex as much as you do, or when they don't seem as attracted to you or desirous of you as before.

Normally, when a relationship begins, we don't feel the little rejections because we may be so "in love" that we do not see each other clearly.

Or we are on our best behavior—open and available because the feelings are so strong and so fresh.

But once the fears begin to set in, the disappointments follow.

Most relationships become a series of little rejections and abandonments, one after the other.

How do we deal with this?

It is important for us to understand that these situations trigger our abandonment wound.

We enter into all our significant relationships with the hunger to receive the kind of unconditional love that we did not receive as a child.

More specifically, we are hungering for precisely those basic needs to be met that were not met before.

For instance, if you did not feel supported in developing your creativity and discovering and exploring your basic life energies (such as sexuality) as a child, you will be hungry to receive that from your intimate partner.

And not only will you be hungering to receive this support, you will be especially sensitive to the moments when you don't!

You will become highly disturbed when you feel unsupported, and you will very likely become very angry if you feel repressed in expressing and living your energy.

The same is true if as a child you lacked the loving and attentive presence of your mother or father.

Then you will hunger for this kind of presence today and if you feel that it is not there, you may react strongly with anger and disappointment.

We are most sensitive to those needs that we did not have filled as children and will feel unloved and abandoned when we feel that these needs are not being met today.

Let's take a moment to look at the basic needs that we all had as children.

1. The need to feel wanted and received in love.

2. The need to feel special and respected as a unique person.

3. The need to have your basic natural feelings validated and supported (for example, sadness, anger, fear, pain, and insecurity).

4. The need to be validated and encouraged to discover your unique energy (for example, passion, sexuality, creativity, power, joy, resourcefulness, silence and solitude).

5. The need to feel safe, secure, and protected.

6. The need to be physically touched with loving presence.

7. The need to be inspired and motivated to learn and to develop your natural gifts and a strong sense of yourself.

8. The need to know that it is OK to make mistakes and to learn from your mistakes.

9. The need to witness love, intimacy, and respect from your caregivers.

10. The need to be encouraged and supported to separate from your parents or caregivers.

11. The need to receive loving limits and to be disciplined with loving communication and respect; without violence or threats.

Because some or many of our basic needs were not met as children, we believe that in order to be happy today, we have to find someone or something to meet those needs—that we have to satisfy our hunger for these needs from the outside.

Perhaps we project that hunger on a person, or perhaps we use a substance or activity such as alcohol, drugs, shopping, entertainment, the Internet, or eating to fulfill that need.

But that only brings us deeper suffering because another person, substance, or activity cannot fill the hole.

Actually, the secret is that once we deeply validate our basic needs—those which were unmet when we were children and those which we still hunger for today—and we feel and accept the pain and emptiness, and honor that these are still basic needs, *that is enough.*

It is as if that place inside just needs to be felt and seen and then something changes.

Then we are nourishing ourselves and giving ourselves what we so deeply miss.

Exercise: Exploring Your Basic Needs

Take a moment to read over the list above.

As you read each one, notice if this need is important to you now in your relationships.

Notice if you are aware of this need and how deep it is.

Ask yourself,

"How was this need met or not met when I was a child?"

"How did I feel when it was not met?"

"How did I deal with missing this basic need?"

Allow yourself to feel what you missed and to honor that this is still a deep need inside.

CHAPTER 5:

WHY DO WE REPEAT PATTERNS THAT CREATE REJECTION?

There is no coincidence in the kind of people we attract to fall in love with.

It is conditioned by the ways that our parents related to us and by the way we approach love in our lives today.

Remember Suzanne from the introduction?

She was furious with her boyfriend because he wanted to sleep with other women. When she was a child, her father was an alcoholic and could not take care of the family emotionally or financially. Suzanne learned early on that men could not be trusted. Deep inside, she did not feel worth. All the men she had been with had betrayed her by abusing drugs and alcohol and sleeping with other women. She could not see that she was attracted to men just like her father. What she also had trouble seeing was that deep inside she was angry with men and full of expectations that only drove men away from her.

This tendency to repeat this pattern and the buried feelings of rage for being abandoned as a child are very deep. The way our parents and especially our opposite-sex parent treated us is how we understand love. It is what we know, what we expect, and what we believe we deserve.

Here are some more examples:

Angelina had always been attracted to men who were physically and financially strong, giving the impression of being confident, but underneath were basically only interested in themselves. Then they rejected her for newer, more exciting pastures in order to make new conquests. Her father behaved the same way when she was a child (and still does)! But she idealized men like this.

Antony was attracted to women who were submissive, eager to please, and compliant. Then he became abusive and demanding, just the way his father treated his mother. The women would finally leave him because they could not stand his disrespectful behavior.

Matthew attracted women who were dominating, caretaking, super-responsible, and controlling. His mother was similar. He liked to have his girlfriends take charge, but would complain that they treated him as a child.

There are many such patterns, and often they are not so easy to recognize.

On the surface, the pattern we create is most similar to how our opposite-sex parent behaved and treated us.

But in fact, these patterns reflect a complex mixture of what we received from both parents and what we learned deep inside about how men and women relate to each other.

In essence, they are based on:

- What we *learned about love* from experiences of being loved or not loved as a child.

- What we learned about *how to be a man or a woman.*

- What we came *to feel about ourselves as a person and as a man or woman.*

- And what we *believe about love.*

From how we were treated as children, we may have come to believe that love does not exist, or that we don't deserve it, or that no one will be able to give us what we need. We may have come to believe that men must provide for women's every needs, or vice versa.

Or, we may have decided:

- "If I open, I will be mistreated."

- "Love only leads to conflict, disappointment, and pain."

- "I have to take care of myself; it is not wise to depend on anyone else."

- "For me to open, I have to be sure that the other person can be totally available."

- "I don't believe that if I open, I can still have my own space."

- "I am not really worthy of being loved."

- "Whenever I open myself, I will get misunderstood, rejected, or abused."

- "Living together with someone is boring."

These beliefs about love are based on the role models of our early childhoods.

They are based on what we observed happening between our parents and on how we were seen and treated.

At those moments so long ago, we made some profound decisions, many of which have remained deeply embedded in our unconscious.

These decisions now will rule our lives unless we bring them into awareness and explore them.

And because we are seldom aware of them, we behave unconsciously out of them.

We react from our beliefs about love.

We attract people who will validate these beliefs.

If our childhoods included abuse, that is what we are attracted to.

If we experienced neglect and deprivation of our basic needs, that is what we will be attracted to.

Exercise: What is Your Concept of Love?

Based on your experience as a child, take a moment to ask yourself about your deepest beliefs regarding what to expect of love.

- Do you believe that you are worthy of love?

- Do you believe that another person is capable of loving you?

- Do you believe that you will always be disappointed in the end?

- What do you have to do to receive love: give, or be?

- Do you believe that "the right person" is waiting for you and it is just a matter of time?

- Do you believe that you will never find "the right person?"

Notice whether your experiences in relationships have validated and reinforced these beliefs.

CHAPTER 6:

"ABANDONMENT AND SHAME GO SHOPPING"

Most of us enter into and remain in relationships in what we call *the wounded-child state-of-consciousness.*

First of all, we often enter into a relationship in a childish state of thinking.

We call it *abandonment goes shopping* because we are behaving from our wounded child and that strongly influences the responses we get from those we come close to.

For instance, this childish state of thinking unconsciously may say:

"I am looking for someone who will take away my fears and loneliness."

"I am looking for someone who will be unconditionally respectful of my needs, borders, and integrity without my having to say or do anything."

Even though we are now adults, much of the time, we do not act or think like adults at all, especially when we enter into or are in a relationship.

We are thinking and behaving like entitled and mystified children. This entitled/mystified child dreams, hopes, and expects.

We do not see life or the other person at all clearly because our hopes, dreams, and expectations blind us.

And from this wounded-child state-of-consciousness, we recreate the same patterns over and over again.

The best way to identify our pattern is to get to know how our wounded inner child thinks, feels, and behaves when we begin or are in a relationship.

In the beginning of a relationship, our wounded child's mystified thinking can be:

- "I have found the love of my life—my perfect soul mate, the one I have been waiting my whole life for."

- "This person is totally perfect—so sensitive, strong, alive, passionate, intelligent, and so on."

- "If this person loves me, then he or she will be there for me, and will be kind, respectful, and giving. This person will be extremely sensitive to my feelings and needs."

- "We will be happy forever."

- "I will never be lonely again."

- "We are so alike, it is unbelievable."

- "This is the best sex I have ever had, and it will last forever."

Mystified and entitled thinking comes from our wounded child, who lives in a fantasy world.

The wounded child pretends that life is a fairy tale where the prince and princess live happily ever after, and pain, loneliness, rejection, fear, and boredom are gone forever.

Once we have entered into a relationship, this entitled and mystified thinking will powerfully influence our behavior.

For instance:

- We are absolutely convinced that someone who says he or she loves us *should behave in certain ways.*

- When our expectations are not met, we *feel deeply betrayed.*

- When our expectations are not met, we can *demand, throw tantrums, get insanely jealous, withdraw, or sink into despair and resignation.*

- We *play power games and use strategies* of control, and use manipulation to get what we want because it is what we have always done and we see no other way.

- We habitually *take revenge* when we feel hurt.

But mystified and entitled thinking is not the only way that our wounded child controls our life.

We also may have deep and crippling *shame thinking* which directs our behavior.

This is another aspect of our wounded-child state that thinks and behaves in a way that determines who we attract as lovers and how we attract them.

For instance:

- "I can't believe that this person likes or loves me! *Why me?*"

- "I am not *good enough* for this person."

- "Maybe I will not be *a good enough lover.*"

- "I have *to prove* that I am a good enough lover."

- "If this person *finds out my secrets*, then he or she won't love me anymore."

- "If this person treats me *without respect, that's what I deserve.*"

We call this *shame shopping* because our thinking and behavior are directed by feelings of unworthiness.

And once we are in a relationship, this shame thinking also has a profound affect on our lives.

- We *cannot express or even feel our needs.*

- We are convinced that it is too good to last; something bad is going to happen.

- We believe that we don't deserve happiness.

- We *compromise* ourselves and give away our power because our fears of rejection or abuse are so strong.

- We may *accept* humiliation and abuse because it is what we feel we deserve.

- We can't *set limits* because we may not even be aware that our boundaries have been violated.

There are an endless amount of behaviors that are motivated by entitled, mystified, frightened, and insecure wounded parts of us.

And the trouble is that this behavior creates exactly what we fear and at the same time expect.

For instance, Anna, a client of ours, entered into a relationship with a man who seemed to be the man of her dreams. She saw him as physically handsome, streetwise, entertaining, charismatic, and a super-lover. For several months, they had a wonderful time together and she considered getting married and moving in together. He told her that he also had been waiting to be with someone like her and that he loved that she inspired him to grow emotionally and spiritually.

However, at one point, he told her that he could not be monogamous and he began to make love with other women. He was honest about it, but his honesty moved into humiliation. At a party they attended together, he flirted with a woman and then went into a bedroom to have sex with her.

Anna had been continually humiliated by her mother and she had become used to this kind of treatment. When we asked her how she felt when her boyfriend abused her in this way at the party, she replied that she knew he was "like this" but loved him anyway. She was willing to accept this kind of behavior because in her wounded state, she expected it and could not imagine someone loving her enough to behave respectfully. She still considered marrying and moving in with him.

This example may not resonate with you, but most of us will behave irrationally and inappropriately in many different ways in our relationships.

What is important to understand is that by behaving from our wounded child, we determine what will happen later in the relationship and we program our rejection.

It is as if we are sending out a message to the other person to reject us and humiliate us.

Or our demands and expectations push him or her away.

Or we are so accustomed to pulling away and not communicating that the other person eventually leaves out of frustration.

Our unworthiness, our avoidance of intimacy, our anger, control strategies, dependencies, giving ourselves away for love—all of these patterns invite rejection eventually.

It is impossible for our wounded child to set limits and so we run over ourselves, feel resentful, and eventually close off and pull away.

Here's another example:

A woman was sharing with us that her relationships with men had always involved her feeling abused sexually.

"I feel that men take advantage of me and make love the way they want without feeling what I want."

"What happens to you when they are doing that?" we asked.

"I always go along with it and often I end up feeling disgusted. Then sooner or later I leave the relationship."

When we begin to identify and explore these negative beliefs, expectations, and behaviors, we can see how they drive the patterns that we may find ourselves in.

Why We Create Rejection

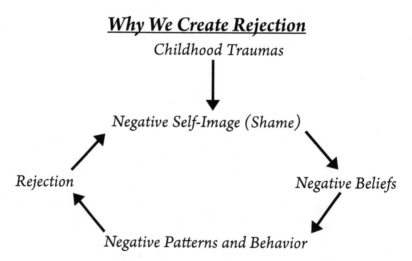

Childhood Traumas

Negative Self-Image (Shame)

Rejection

Negative Beliefs

Negative Patterns and Behavior

Exercise: Exploring Your Patterns that Create Rejection

Take a moment to consider your most intimate relationship. Ask yourself:

- What are your *beliefs* about how you need to behave with this person?

- Do you *think* that you *deserve* to be loved by this person?

- How do you *feel* about yourself when you are with this person?

- How do you *feel* inside when you are with this person?

- What do you notice about how you *behave* when you are with this person—do you compromise, beg, demand, expect, or get angry or pull away when you don't get what you want?

- Is it difficult for you to feel your own needs when you are with this person?

CHAPTER 7:

WHAT ARE REJECTION FEELINGS AND HOW CAN WE BE WITH THEM?

Rejection, loss, and abandonment provoke many different feelings.

What we feel and how we deal with what we feel depends very much on our emotional makeup.

I (Krish) remember that at one time in my life, I was rejected by three women in the space of a year. I felt utterly insecure and unworthy. But the separation that was most difficult for me to overcome was when my first significant relationship ended. At that time, I was frozen and depressed. I felt listless, I lacked motivation to get on with my life, and I did not have the tools to understand what was happening.

When we get rejected, we may feel *panic and shock, guilt and shame, anger, rage, depression, despair, deep sadness, and grief— one at a time, all of them at once, or different feelings over time.*

How many of these feelings did you feel the last time you experienced a rejection?

There is no predictable order to these feelings.

But it is important to be aware of all of them.

They are most strong when someone leaves us or when we lose a loved one.

They also come up with the little rejections and abandonments that we discussed in chapter 4.

1. Shock and Fear

When we get rejected, often the first experience is one of intense *panic* and/or *shock*.

The pain is so great that our nervous system either becomes highly activated and disturbed, or it simply shuts down.

We feel overloaded, and the most natural response to these overwhelming feelings of rejection and loss is to feel panic or shock.

With *panic*, we might sense a rapid heart rate; shortness of breath; shaking or trembling; speaking quickly or loudly; sweaty palms; cold extremities; compulsive, repetitive, or rapid thinking; feelings of doom as if something terrible is about to happen; restlessness; hyperactivity; and the inability to relax.

Shock (or frozen fear) on the other hand, is a state of immobilization. We freeze. We cannot feel; sometimes we cannot move, speak, or even think clearly.

We may shut down the feelings so completely that we don't feel anything. It becomes like a permanent numbness.

We may notice shallow breathing, feeling numb, or our minds rambling with repetitive thoughts.

We might notice pains in the body, or that we are watching ourselves as if in a movie, feeling far away, not present in our bodies, and unable to breathe.

We may notice that we cannot concentrate, or we don't hear or understand other people well, or we become forgetful and even unable to perform the most simple of tasks.

Or we move through life automatically, not being present in the actions.

We may notice that we are disconnecting from our feelings, any feelings—and perhaps also from other people's feelings.

Or we may notice that we are emotional in a way that seems excessive, at least to other people, or very unusual for us.

Most of us have dealt with abandonment and loss in this way from a very early age.

After all, how else can a small child cope with one or both of his parents not being present emotionally, or one or both not being present physically?

It is for this reason that we are seldom aware how profoundly we have been abandoned as children.

We did not feel it when it was happening because we were in shock.

So, today, when faced again with the terrible pain of loss, we respond the way we always have.

2. Shame and Guilt

When we get rejected, we feel terrible.

We usually feel horribly *guilty, or even worse, deep shame and unworthiness.*

We might feel guilty because we failed—once again.

Or we might judge that we were not sensitive, alive, intelligent, passionate, caring, or responsible enough.

When someone rejects us, it can plunge us into thinking that we made terrible mistakes, we never do anything right, we are not good enough lovers, and so on.

Rejection activates our inner critics, who powerfully attack us with condemning critical voices that we believe to be true.

These voices may be similar to actual attacks and criticisms that came to us from parents, teachers, or other students in our childhoods.

Even when we experience loss without actual rejection, we can also feel shame.

We may tell ourselves that we missed a deeper connection with the person, that there were things we would have liked to say but never did, that we would have wanted to spend more quality time together, and tell that person how much we cared for her or him.

Shame feelings come with a loss of energy and motivation, and feelings of hopelessness, uselessness, and that life has no meaning.

It may even become hard to get out of bed in the morning.

And the more strongly we believe the critical, judging voices inside, the deeper the shame.

When the shame hits us, it is important to get support from someone who can help us to see that our inner critic is not speaking the truth.

That person can be a close and trusted friend, or perhaps, it needs to be a therapist who knows how to give us perspective and insight about our shame.

I (Krish) could not get the support I needed just from friends. I needed to have someone to talk to who was able to feel and understand what I was going through, something that only a skilled therapist could give me.

3. Anger or Rage

Rejection or loss can also provoke powerful anger.

We are angry with ourselves for losing ourselves, for not trusting our intuition, for giving away our power, or for compromising and allowing ourselves to be disrespected.

But we can also feel a kind of primitive rage toward the other person for rejecting us.

"How could this person do this to me?"

"I cannot accept that this person has rejected me!"

Our anger is often a defense against feeling the pain and the shame of rejection.

Even the little rejections that we spoke about in an earlier chapter can trigger this rage.

It is almost intolerable to feel the humiliation when someone rejects us.

We want to avoid feeling this at all costs, and one of the ways we do that is to get angry.

When we don't get the attention, love, approval, warmth, or unconditional love that we yearn for, it triggers very deep anger from earlier times when we did not get these needs met.

In these moments, we want to give the pain back and we naturally direct it at the person who has rejected us or is rejecting us now.

It is healthy to feel the anger and it is an important step of our healing.

But it is essential to know that the person who rejected or left us today has only triggered the anger of abandonment and rejection that happened early in our lives.

In fact, this is anger that we could not feel as a child, when it was so painful to not get some or all of our basic needs met.

So, it is important, if the anger wakes up, to direct this anger toward the place where the trauma came from—our caretakers, teachers, siblings, and other students or friends.

There is anger for the injustice of having been deprived of basic needs for security, love, support, caring, support, approval, and appreciation.

There is the anger for having being shamed, invaded, and abused emotionally, physically, sexually, or spiritually.

When we don't feel this rage, we can easily feel guilty and deserving of the abandonment or abuse we received. Or we get depressed.

Rather than repress our anger or throw it toward the person whom we feel has rejected or abandoned us today, it is important to feel the energy in the body.

When we tune in to the energy of anger in the body, we might become aware of heat, tightness in the solar plexus or elsewhere, or tension in the fists or jaw.

The one and only purpose of working with our anger is to reclaim our empowerment and the ability to feel self-love—knowing that we are loved and we deserve to give and receive love.

In feeling our anger we reclaim our strength and the ability to protect ourselves today.

4. Depression and Despair

It is common that we might sink into depression and despair when we lose someone or when someone leaves us, or when we are not getting the love and appreciation that we want from someone.

We get depressed because we don't have the tools to understand and integrate what is happening to us.

We feel like giving up because we cannot make sense out of all the pain and confusion inside.

When we get rejected or lose someone it opens an emptiness inside.

It opens up this deep inner hole in our being and often we do not know how to handle the pain and the shock.

Then we can easily give up and feel despair.

The difficulty with depression and despair is that it feels like there is no way out. We feel terrible inside and terrible about ourselves for being depressed.

We feel deep shame and we know that no one wants to be with us when we feel this way.

So not only is there shame, but there are also loneliness and isolation.

It helps to know that:

- Rejection and abandonment have roots in the past.

- Feeling the shame heals it.

- We can learn and grow from this experience.

- Moving the body and connecting with nature supports us in this difficult time.

5. Sadness and Grief

When we begin to allow ourselves to feel the sadness of loss and rejection, we are taking a big step to recovering and coming back to ourselves.

There is great sadness when someone leaves us.

It is like a death.

Inside, we may be aware that the relationship is over.

But it can be very hard to accept this final truth.

Often much of our behavior and thinking is because we don't want to face it and accept it.

Holding onto hope prevents us from feeling the pain of the death of the relationship.

There are many aspects and layers to our grief:

- First, letting go of hope and feeling our helplessness to bring our loved one back.

- Second, we need to feel the pain of the hole that this person's leaving has opened inside.

- Third, we have to feel the sadness of a child (our inner child) who has a lifetime history of feeling abandoned in many different ways.

- We have to feel the sadness of a child (again our inner child) who was shamed and made to feel unworthy of love and who lost the love for himself or herself.

- We have to feel the sadness of a child who lost his or her innocence and trust in the goodness of life, the abundance of love, and the caring of others.

- We have to feel the sadness and pain of all the ways we have hurt other people because of our loss of trust.

All of this is the grief work.

The power of all of these feelings—shock, panic, shame, anger, despair, or sadness - depends on how much we have worked with the abandonment wound, and how much we understand and feel about the connection between past and present rejections.

It is not possible to predict which of these five feelings will be strongest for us, nor is it possible to predict in what order they will come up as time goes on.

All that we can suggest is to give space to all of them and learn how to deal with them by reaching out for help.

Often they seem overwhelming, confusing, and meaningless.

You might say to yourself:

- "I can't understand where all this panic is coming from."

- "What is the point of feeling all this pain and sadness?"

- "It's too much; I can't handle this."

- "What's the point of being sad? I need to make myself happy and enjoy life again."

- "There is no end to it if I allow these feelings."

- "I should be over it by now."

This is all coming from the voice of your wounded child who does not want to accept the situation and feel the pain.

Instead, we can choose to stop, and take time to go in and actually feel the body.

When we are taking care to observe our body experience with gentle scrutiny, something quite magical happens.

When attached unconsciously to our negative thoughts, the feelings intensify as though we are pouring fire on them and giving them new life.

But if we can pull our awareness away from the thoughts and stay with the body, our nervous system settles.

Just by staying with the pain or the emptiness in the body, as sensations in the body, leads us to relaxation.

Slowly, we come back to the moment and discover, at least for a while, that we are OK.

Yes, the pain returns.

Rejection pain comes in waves.

But each wave slowly gets easier to feel and be with, and then over time becomes less intense.

Slowly, our hearts heal.

Exercise: Being with Our Rejection Feelings

Bring to mind the last time that you felt rejected or abandoned. (You can also think of the last time that you did not get what you wanted from someone very close to you.)

- Did or do you go into *shock*?—unable to feel your body, feeling confused, feeling paralyzed.

- Did or do you experience *shame*?—judging yourself with harsh inner critical voices, feeling a lack of motivation, and feelings of unworthiness.

- Did or do you feel *anger*?—anger at the person for rejecting you, wanting to take revenge, wanting to see the other person suffer like you have suffered or are suffering, anger at other people in your life who have hurt you.

- Did or do you feel *depressed*?—feeling low energy, unable to function in your life, feeling hopeless and meaningless, and believing the negative voices in your head.

- Did or do you feel *sadness*?—sadness for the loss of this person, sadness for all the beautiful times you had together that are no longer there, sadness for your own past experiences of being rejected and abused.

Now, gently, close your eyes and allow yourself to relax.

Imagine that the moment of rejection is happening right now. (Perhaps it is.)

Take a deep breath.

Gently observe your body.

Notice, first the quality of the feeling.

Is it anger, sadness, panic, or shock (frozenness)?

Take some time to feel the subtle physical sensations connected to what is happening inside.

Observe the sensations and feelings closely without trying to change them. As you do, see if something slowly changes by itself.

After ten minutes, notice how you are feeling.

CHAPTER 8:

DEALING WITH THE NEGATIVE MIND

We have already mentioned some of the negative thoughts that come up when we get rejected.

Our minds can be our worst enemies when we are experiencing an abandonment or rejection crisis.

The thoughts eat away at our self-esteem, our motivation, our trust in the future, and even our trust in life itself.

The problem is not so much that we have these negative thoughts, but that we believe them.

How can we deal with all this negative thinking?

First of all, it is important to know that we cannot control or silence the negative mind, especially when an event as strong as a rejection triggers us.

But we can learn to get some distance from these thoughts.

The first step in creating distance is to become acutely aware what our negative mind is saying to us and actually writing the thoughts down so that we can see them in front of us.

In our work, we teach that there are two ways to evaluate a negative thought—a critical or condemning thought about ourselves, others, or life in general.

One way—the normal, habitual, conditioned, and familiar way—is to believe it.

For example, here are four common negative thoughts:

- "I deserve to be rejected because I am not worthy of being loved."

- "I can't trust anyone because other people are not sensitive or caring enough."

- "I will never find another person who is so right for me."

- "I should have done more to make that person love me."

When we listen from the inner judge or inner critic, we believe these thoughts to be true.

And we take the recent experience of rejection as proof.

But what if we could switch channels and listen to these thoughts from a different space?

We call this other channel *listening to the inner wisdom* or *listening from the heart.*

When we hear, "I deserve to be rejected because I am not worthy of being loved," our *inner wisdom* could say to us, "That is your shame talking. This experience was a lesson to help you learn to love yourself more deeply. Perhaps you can explore what you learned about your needs and your old patterns from this experience."

When we hear, "I can't trust anyone because other people are not sensitive or caring enough," our inner wisdom could say, "Your early childhood experiences taught you to mistrust. Perhaps you have chosen someone very similar to your early experience of relating. What have you learned about what you need now to open and trust?"

When we hear, "I will never find another person who is right for me," our inner wisdom might say, "You are only learning what is right for you. Probably, this person was not right for you because otherwise, you would still be with her or him. You have no idea what existence has in store for you. For now, just focus on learning what this experience was meant to teach you about love and relating."

When we hear, "I should have done more to make this person love me," your wisdom could say, "At the time, there was nothing you could have done differently. Seek help to guide you through the pain of this experience so that you can let go. If it is meant for you to be with this person, it is not in your control. Trust in life and learn from this experience."

Our inner wisdom sees the bigger picture and looks at every situation from the perspective of compassionate understanding.

It knows that our life is a journey of awakening, of healing our wounds, and that relationships that end with a rejection occur because there is some very important lesson that we need to learn to become a whole and mature person.

As we mentioned earlier, often, in the child state of consciousness and before we have identified this state of consciousness, we create relationships from a space of wanting to escape from our fears and pain.

As we said before, we seek out partners in a fantasy state, hoping that finding "the one" will mean we are never alone, frightened, or insecure ever again.

And that is exactly what creates rejection.

In our deepest wisdom we know that we want more out of life than escape and fantasy.

We want more than using another person to shelter us from the pains of life, because otherwise we can never grow up and become a real person.

We will remain children forever.

When we are rejected, or even when we are in a relationship, and we feel frustrated and disappointed that we are not getting what we want, our inner wisdom knows that this is an opportunity to grow, to learn, and to reclaim our dignity.

Exercise: Transforming Our Negative Thoughts

When you are experiencing either a big or a little rejection, examine closely the negative thoughts you have about yourself, about the other person, or about life in general.

Write them down.

Then imagine that you are listening to those thoughts from a space of inner wisdom, from your heart.

See if your inner wisdom has a different interpretation of the rejection.

Listen to what it says to you and write it down.

CHAPTER 9:

ACTING OUT OR ACTING IN

What do you *do* when you feel rejected?

Do you blame, get angry, complain, play the "poor me" role, get busy, eat chocolate, smoke, drink, give up, or pretend you don't care?

When we experience abandonment or rejection, our first and deeply instinctual reaction is to do anything not to feel the pain.

This is called either *acting out or acting in.*

Acting out includes all our efforts to undo what has happened— all our strategies of distraction, denial, or avoidance of feeling. It includes all the ways we try to change the other person, blaming, attacking, accusing, or even moving into some addiction to not feel the pain.

Acting in is the way that we attack ourselves for what has happened and become lost in guilt, shame, and self-destructive thoughts and behavior. This also includes collapsing, giving up, and moving into depression.

In these moments, our wounded child has taken over our lives.

This part of us does not have the strength or the resources to deal with the pain of rejection.

It does not have the inner space to contain the pain.

And so it moves into a strategy to take the pain away.

These strategies apply equally for a big or a little rejections, either the loss of a love or the frustration of not having our needs met.

In fact, in some ways our strategies are stronger when we feel frustrated in a relationship because they can become habitual ways that we act toward our partners.

Here are some common acting-out strategies:

1. Bargaining

One common strategy is *bargaining.* We want to do anything to try to get the person back—beg, persuade, or try to impress on him or her that we have changed, and that we are now willing to give what he or she wants.

For instance, can you remember a time when you were rejected and you felt compelled to call the other person? You were feeling so lonely and rejected and you were convinced that if you could just hear her or his voice, it would be enough.

Or it would be enough just to meet the person again.

Bargaining also includes the habits of being compliant, compromising, submissive, and collapsed while in a relationship—giving up our power for the sake of harmony, and the fear of aggression or rejection.

2. Revenge

Another acting-out strategy is *planning* or even *taking revenge.* You become obsessed with what you can do to hurt the person who rejected you or who has hurt you.

We have known some amazing cases of what injured partners have done to take revenge.

One woman went out and made love to her ex-partner's best friends and then called him to let him know what she did, giving him details of their sexual encounters.

One man cut up all his girlfriend's favorite clothes when she left him for another man.

One woman called the new girlfriend of her ex-partner and told her how great their sex had been.

We often say that when we are rejected or hurt, our wounded child inside is not happy until he or she sees blood.

Our strategies are not rational, considerate, or kind.

They are driven by a history of shame and hurt that we have buried inside and built up inside for years.

3. *Aggression and Raging*

A third and very common form of acting out is *overt aggression* and *raging*.

We use anger not to feel pain.

We feel justified in feeling anger toward the person who has rejected or hurt us.

We even feel anger, although it is often unconscious, toward someone who has died and abandoned us.

As we said earlier, it is natural to feel this anger, but it is destructive to feel justified in throwing that anger on the person who rejected or hurt us.

The energy in itself is healthy, for a number of reasons.

- Anger is necessary for us to set limits and stand up for ourselves, and reconnecting with this energy is empowering.

- The rejection experience has awakened the anger that has been buried inside for all the hurts we received in our lives. That awakening is good.

- The energy of anger protects us from sinking into depression and resignation, which is the unhealthiest form of acting in. (We will say more about this in a moment.)

- We can use the energy of anger to wake up the memories of past insults and traumas, and in doing so bring back our vitality and passion for life.

The healing movement is to allow yourself to *feel* the anger toward the person who has rejected or abandoned you, but then rather than *acting it out on that person*, feel it and see where it comes from in your past.

Then find ways of expressing this anger in a healthy, contained, and appropriate way such as in a workshop, with a therapist, in a martial arts class, or any other form of structured activity that motivates and encourages you to feel and express this energy in a safe place where you are not hurting yourself or someone else.

4. Bitterness

If we do not take the healing step described above, we repress our anger, and instead of feeling the rage and the anger, we go into *bitterness*. This is a highly self-destructive way of acting in pain.

With bitterness, we harbor the anger inside and feel alienated from other people and from life. We get lost in believing that love does not exist, that people are against us, that the world is a cold and unloving place.

It is like emotional cancer that eats away at us inside, isolating us, and causing other people to distance themselves from us.

Sometimes we are holding bitterness from a rejection that has happened years ago.

The only way out of bitterness is to get help with feeling how our hearts have closed, to feel the pain of the isolation we have created for ourselves, and to go back to the experience of the rejection that hurt so much and feel the shame, pain, and anger.

5. Resignation

A close cousin to bitterness is *resignation.*

With resignation, we decide, consciously or unconsciously, to give up on life and love.

This is a highly painful state, although in the state of resignation we are numb to the pain.

We are avoiding dealing with what is happening to us.

We have closed our doors and turned away from life and love.

Sometimes it takes a friend or a good therapist to wake us up out of resignation.

One way that helps us come out of resignation is to move the body—physical exercise, sports, martial arts, kickboxing, running, training at a gym, active meditation—anything that gets the life energy moving again.

Sometimes if someone can simply commit to something like this for an hour twice or three times a week, it takes him or her out of the resignation and depression.

Recovering from rejection takes time.

It can be the most painful experience in the world.

6. *Addictions and Other Self-Destructive Behaviors*

Perhaps the most common way of acting in comes in the form of *addiction.*

Of all the ways we have mentioned, this is perhaps the most universal way we avoid feeling the pain of rejection and abandonment.

We may choose alcohol, cocaine, marijuana, coffee, food, sex, sweets, or cigarettes. We might even become addicted to shopping, television, or socializing—anything that takes us away from feeling the pain.

One client of ours drank three vodkas a night for months after a woman left him.

Another client began smoking two packs of cigarettes a day.

When rejection strikes, our nervous system become so disturbed and so activated, that we will try to find anything to calm it down.

The substances that we turn to are an effort to get some relaxation and some relief from the fear and the pain. It is a way we try to soothe ourselves.

We can also turn to activities for relief and distraction, such as becoming excessively engaged in work or even sports.

It is not uncommon for someone who has been rejected to go to sex for instant gratification—seeking out as many sexual partners as he or she can, going to bars, picking up prostitutes, or masturbating to Internet pornography.

It is important to be gentle with ourselves when we notice that we are dealing with the pain of abandonment or rejection by distracting ourselves with activities or substances.

But it is serious when this becomes a lifestyle pattern.

In addition, addictive behavior is often combined with self-critical thoughts. We berate and judge ourselves continuously, taking the blame for whatever goes wrong, comparing ourselves endlessly with others, or feeling that we have done something horribly wrong.

Exercise: Investigating Your Acting-Out Behaviors

If you are facing rejection or abandonment right now in your life or in your past, either the big or little kind, take a moment to ask yourself: "Which of the six acting-out or acting-in behaviors do I or did I go into?"

1. *Bargaining and Begging*

2. *Revenge*

3. *Aggression or Rage*

4. *Bitterness*

5. *Resignation and Depression*

6. *Addiction and Distraction*

What did each of these behaviors feel like and how did they make you feel about yourself?

What response did you get from others?

How long did it last? Or are you still in one or more of these behaviors?

CHAPTER 10:

CHRONIC ACTING OUT

A client of ours is convinced that men are brutes. She has been in many relationships, but nearly always leaves them complaining that men are too insensitive and not willing to grow up. In lovemaking, she has a habit of doing what doesn't feel right for her because she feels responsible to "give him pleasure." Then she resents the man for being a selfish lover. She has never found a man who is strong and sensitive enough for her.

By not standing up for herself, then getting enraged and categorizing men as "brutes," she is pushing them away. Her standards and her conclusions about men have become her defenses against opening to love.

Another client of ours embraced a philosophy called being "polyamorous," which meant that he chose to have many sexual partners and saw this as the most creative and growthful way of relating. Going deeper into his personal story, we discovered that he was continually controlled and manipulated by his depressive mother and abandoned at an early age by his father. This philosophy served to shield him from having to face his deep fears of opening to one woman and running the risk of being controlled and manipulated.

We worked with a woman who had a pattern of being attracted to and entering into relationships with charismatic, narcissistic men whom she idealized, while feeling inadequate and undeserving of their love. Eventually, they would reject her and she would pursue another man who fit the same criteria.

These are all examples of what we call *chronic acting out*—points of view or ongoing behaviors that serve to shelter us from having to feel the pain of rejection and abandonment from our childhoods and repeating these experiences in our lives today.

There are four major forms of chronic acting out. In each of these ways, our wounded child is taking our basic unmet needs for love, acceptance, and connection, and doing something to avoid opening to love.

1. Avoidance

One common way is to avoid intimacy altogether.

Perhaps we have built lifestyles in which we don't have time to spend with others, or we limit our involvements to casual sexual encounters.

Or we believe that we cannot find partners who fill our expectations.

This avoids the pain of a rejection that cuts deeply inside because we have not opened our vulnerability to other people.

Peter, for example, had created a lifestyle in which he had many sexual encounters but rarely stayed with one woman longer than a few months. When he fell in love with Beatrice, he resolved to commit and stop being with other women. But he found it very difficult to stay open to Beatrice, so instead of running away by making love to other women, he found himself devoting large amounts of time to his training as a marathon runner, working long hours at the office, or working at home on the computer. As one might imagine, this left Beatrice highly frustrated and they began quarreling. He felt she was being too demanding and she felt that he was simply finding new and different ways to avoid facing his fears of closeness.

2. Dependency

Another common way of chronically acting out from our fears rather than facing them is to create relationships that have no real depth but have become arrangements of mutual security.

There are many relationships like this that provide a nice home, a comfortable lifestyle, financial security, and mutual dependency of two people being together but not really growing and facing their fears.

Annette, a woman we have worked with, offers a good example of this style. She is deeply unhappy in her marriage, feels that her husband is insensitive, aggressive, not attuned to the children, concerned with his own needs and wants, and a terrible lover. When we asked her why she stays with him, her response was, "I have to stay for the sake of the children and because I do not believe that I could find anything better."

A variety of this style of acting out is to hope or expect the other person to meet our needs and take away our loneliness and survival fears.

We may hold the belief that our happiness depends on this.

Then once we are in a relationship, we become deeply dependent, lose ourselves, rely on our partners, and perhaps complain when they are not doing more to make us feel secure and loved.

Part of this form of acting out is to have many *expectations* for how the other person should behave.

The problem is not that we have the expectations, because we all do.

The problem is that we *believe* in our expectations—that our partners *should* be this way and should do this and that these are *natural and reasonable expectations* for a love relationship.

Sylvia, a woman we have worked with, offers a good example of this pattern. She is chronically angry with her boyfriend because he is not "alive" enough. When they are together, she gets upset because he does not want to go to parties with her. She feels that he should be more giving, more energetic, and more present for her. These are her expectations and she is not seeing that he is simply a different person than she is. But on a deeper lever, she is still unable to understand that her complaining about her boyfriend is a shield of her abandonment pain.

3. Addiction

Many of us use addiction as a way of being chronically distracted from our deeper feelings—from our shame and our fears of rejection.

The use of substances or activities can be a way of permanently shielding ourselves from feeling the shame inside and from feeling the depths of our loneliness.

Andrew is a wealthy, fast-living, 49-year-old man who has loved to live "at the edge"—driving fast cars and motorcycles, partying, smoking, and drinking, traveling the world with his many businesses, and enjoying many women. The problem is that some years ago, he fell in love with a woman who cannot tolerate his ways of living and especially his drinking. He has attempted to stop, even going into recovery programs, but he cannot stop. He was motivated to start some deep and consistent therapy work with us because he did not want to lose her. In the process, he discovered that his lifestyle was a deep and unconscious way of avoiding the pain of a difficult childhood. He has not had a drink since he began intensive therapy.

4. Control

Finally, a fourth common form of chronic acting out is control. It can be an automatic, habitual, and unconscious way of attempting to avoid feeling the pain of abandonment by attempting to obsessively control our environment, other people, and even ourselves.

Alicia's husband, Paul, finds it difficult to be with her because he feels that she needs to be in control all the time. When they first came together, things were very different. She was much looser, more flexible, and relaxed. But with time, her controlling behavior became more and more extreme. He feels that she micromanages him, commenting on and criticizing his behavior, requires that their home be spotless and tidy, and worst of all, he claims she supervises his every move in their lovemaking.

Fortunately, Alicia decided to enter into therapy with me (Amana) because she recognized that her controlling behavior was out of control and having destructive effects on her relationship and her life. Slowly, we uncovered her underlying fears and pain of being raised by a mother who was schizophrenic and in and out of mental hospitals most of her childhood. Her father dealt with this situation by being absent and involved with his work. She began to recognize that it was never safe for her to lose control because there was simply no one there for her. With time, she was able to take some distance from her needs to control Paul, to feel the fears when she felt out of control, and became able to ask for his support and help instead.

Here are some of the classic situations that provoke one of these four kinds of habitual and chronic acting out.

1. When We Feel Jealous

Jealousy is a very common way to cover our fears of abandonment and rejection.

When your partner does or says or fails to do or say something that provokes these fears, you may find yourself becoming aggressive and raging, demanding explanations, begging for more attention, trying to control his or her actions, invading his or her private space, or threatening or taking revenge.

These reactions may be based on real evidence, or they can be coming simply from your fears.

If you felt rejected, ignored, or neglected in any way as a child, especially from your opposite-sex parent, these fears can be very strong, overpowering, and out of control.

Jealousy can become so painful and troubling that we seek relief through chemicals, drugs, alcohol, or marijuana. Sometimes we just become resigned and depressed.

2. When We Feel Pressure or Expectation

Some of us are highly sensitive to any kind of pressure, expectation, demand, or advice from our partner.

This is especially true if you felt this kind of energy from either or both parents or in school as a child.

Even the suspicion of pressure or expectations can provoke an intense, automatic, immediate, and irrational reaction.

You can get angry and aggressive or you can pull away.

On the other hand, you can become the good boy or girl, or turn into a pleaser or a rescuer. Perhaps later you feel angry and resentful.

But sometimes you have become so used to pleasing as a way of acting out when you feel expectations or demands, that you don't even realize that you have given away your power and your will.

3. *When We Find Something in the Other Person We Want to Change*

When we are close to someone, we would like that person to feel, think, and behave the way we want, or at least in a way that we approve of and understand, because then we feel close to him or her.

But when the other person does something that makes us feel separate and different from him or her, it provokes our abandonment wound.

In that moment we are alone again and we can't relate to the other person.

The way we commonly act out in situations like this is to attempt to change, give advice to, or fix the other person. We may criticize, judge, and nag.

Usually, the other person will not appreciate this behavior because it feels controlling, manipulative, and even aggressive.

The result is often conflict and it creates more distance.

4. *When We Don't Want to Grow Up*

Many of us have a part inside that would rather not have to deal with all the practical details of life—paying taxes, having the car fixed, taking out the garbage, cooking, cleaning, shopping, reading manuals, or even having to go to work every day.

Basically, this part of us does not want to grow up and become responsible.

In a relationship, this part of us that we call *the regressed child,* can easily come out and take over much of our behavior.

Perhaps you notice this part of you in your own life.

It is a common way that we act out in relationships. Perhaps you never thought that this, too, is a cover for our abandonment wound.

Why is that so?

Because the child inside is longing to be taken care of, longing to be protected, and longing for someone to take control of things so that you can relax and play.

Perhaps you missed that freedom in your childhood and you wish you could have it now.

Or perhaps the idea of having to be grown up frightens you and you would rather give that job to your partner.

5. When We Don't Want to Be Vulnerable

The mirror image of the regressed child is *the caretaking child*.

The caretaking child is the one who is always taking care of people, always in control, managing things, and telling others what to do and how to do it.

It seems very mature, but actually it is just another way that our wounded child acts out and covers the abandonment wound.

When you are taking care, rescuing, and being the one in control and always on top of situations, you create dependency in the other person and you avoid feeling dependent and out of control.

When someone feels dependent on you, it is less likely that he or she will reject you.

You might have been abandoned as a child by having to take care of things very early.

You may have learned that this was the way to get love, and you might never have realized that you were forced to give up your playfulness as a child and become an adult much too early.

But in playing the role of the caretaking child, we don't have to be vulnerable and run the risk of being abandoned again.

6. When We Are Making Love

Another situation where you can easily act out to cover your abandonment wound is in sexuality.

Sexuality is an area of our lives that can trigger the deepest feelings of longing and rejection.

It can also give us a wonderful feeling of connection and togetherness, even melting with another person and with life itself.

But it can be deeply disappointing, and when that disappointment arises, we are face-to-face with our abandonment wound.

Rather than feel the pain of this disappointment and realize that it is our abandonment wound, we might easily move into acting out toward our partner with anger, demands, expectations, complaints, pulling away, taking revenge, or becoming depressed or bitter.

Exercise 1: Investigating Your Chronic Ways of Acting Out

Notice if you are using one of these three chronic defenses—avoidance of closeness, dependency, or addiction—as a way of not running the risk of feeling rejected.

How are you doing it?

Exercise 2: Investigating Your Acting Out with "Little Rejections"

In your intimate relationships, what are the ways and situations that you feel disturbed, disappointed, or frustrated?

- How do you feel and react when you are not getting the love, attention, time, or presence that you would like from the other person?

- How do you feel and react when you notice a quality in the other person that you don't like or don't approve of?

- How do you react when you feel controlled or pressured, or have things expected of you?

- What would you like to be different in your sexuality? How do you react to that?

- In what ways would you like your intimate partner to be different? How do you behave about this?

- How does it feel when you notice that he or she is not changing?

- Do you notice yourself feeling and behaving like a child in some situations?

- Do you notice yourself habitually caretaking, rescuing, or giving advice?

CHAPTER 11:

EXPECTATIONS—THE SILENT ESCAPE FROM FACING ABANDONMENT

Expectations are the greatest cause of suffering in our love lives. When we explain this in our work, people are often surprised.

Or they understand what we are saying with their minds, but when faced with a real-life situation, their expectations return in a hurry.

Rachel complains continually about how disappointed she is with her husband. He is not clean, communicative, alive, or sensitive enough, and he is a "poor lover." All her efforts to change him have proven to be hopeless failures.

"Why are you with him?" we ask.

"Because I love him and I cannot imagine a life without him."

"Well," we said, "you have three choices. You can leave him, you can totally accept him the way he is, or you can work together to see if there is some room for growth."

"We were in therapy together for years but nothing really changed," she said.

"Then how is it if you accept him as he is?"

"I can't."

"How is it if you imagine a life without him?" we asked.

"I can't and I don't want to do that."

"OK, you have one other option," we told her. "Your expectations come from your wound of abandonment. If you work with that in groups and in therapy, you will slowly let go of your expectations. And at the same time, make your daily life so full of joy and creativity that you no longer need him to make you happy. But when you complain about him is not an option because it only leads to endless suffering. How does this feel?"

"That last option seems like the best thing for me."

Bringing awareness and understanding to our expectations is a crucial aspect of healing our abandonment wound.

Without knowing it, we go into our relationships full of expectations, fully believing that it is the other person's responsibility to meet them.

We may even define our idea of love as someone who loves us a certain way. Often what draws us to somebody is the belief that our expectations will be met.

Much of the time, we believe that our expectations are totally reasonable and we cling to them like stubborn mules.

Often people in our seminars ask us, "What is the point of being in a relationship if you can't have expectations?"

It is a good question because it shows how deeply conditioned we are to hoping and expecting that we will get what we want from another person.

It is a painful awakening to let go of expectations, or even to see that expectations conflict with seeing people and life as they are.

It means waking up to a world that is not how our emotional child would like it to be.

It is possible that we are not aware how deeply we enter into relationships or live in relationships with expectations because often they may not come up until we get disappointed or frustrated with the other person.

So, one way to examine our expectations is to explore how and where we get disappointed.

Our expectations accurately reflect the ways that we have felt betrayed or invaded as children, and we will be especially sensitive to wanting those needs met that we missed.

For instance, if we experienced one of our parents being emotionally absent as a child, we will expect our lover today to be 100 percent present, and we get frustrated when he or she is not.

It is as if our child inside is saying, "You should be present to me in a way that my parents were not. Finally, I have someone who should give me what I always wanted."

Or, if we felt criticized or given advice to as a child, we will expect and want our friends and lovers not to do the same.

Or, if we had the experience in the past that promises were made to us and not kept, we will expect that they are kept today and will be very sensitive to the times when they are not.

It is perfectly natural that we wish our lovers and close friends to be present and respectful.

But when we hold on to the belief that people should live up to our expectations, we are not able to see and feel our wounds that get triggered when the expectations are not met.

We are then focused on making the other person wrong, and miss the opportunity to feel what is going on inside us when this happens.

We feel righteous and victimized.

When we instead take time to examine our expectations, it is a powerful way to explore our deep wounds of having been betrayed or invaded.

We do not even have to dig around in our past to find out how we were abandoned because we are getting triggered in the here-and-now and can work directly with the trigger to take us back to the wound.

We will attract situations that bring up precisely the ways in which these traumas happened in the past and get reenacted in the present—with our lovers, children, employers, teachers, siblings, parents, and friends.

If we minimize our needs, it may actually seem like we don't have expectations—but we do.

The easiest way to uncover a hidden expectation is to notice when we get irritable.

Behind the irritability is an expectation that was not met. (Next time you go to a restaurant and the food is not any good, notice what happens.)

Another way to notice may be when you suddenly feel depressed and have low energy. This could also show that you had an expectation that was not met by someone close to you.

Here are three simple ways to identify your expectations:

1. Notice what you want from love

Many of us have an idea of love based on how people should feel toward us and treat us. Perhaps we think that if someone loves us, he or she should be considerate and respectful, loving and giving, attentive and attuned to our needs, and committed, faithful, and honest.

These are all important values, but they may not allow us to see the other person for who he or she is. The other person may love you in his or her way, but does not meet your ideas of love.

2. Notice when you get irritable and disturbed by the other person's thoughts, feelings, and behaviors, or how you would like the other person to change

Irritation is always a good barometer of what we want from another person because when we get disturbed, we expect him or her to behave differently.

For instance, we might get irritated that our partner is not as tidy or clean as we would like.

Or we might be upset that he or she is not as sensitive, alive, communicative, adventurous, focused, sexual, or independent as we would like.

If we explore all aspects of our lives—money, food, work, relating, health, entertainment, appearance, home environment, children, parents, marriage, sex, and so forth, we may see how much we expect from other people, especially those closest to us.

3. Notice your opinions and judgments

We all have opinions and we all have judgments.

When we have an opinion or judgment about something, it is because we *expect* things to be a certain way—and just underneath is our abandonment wound.

Often, we don't examine our opinions and our judgments.

We will hold onto them as if we are guarding a precious religion.

But then we never go deeper into ourselves and we don't realize how much our fears of abandonment are running our lives.

When others and life are not as we would like them to be, we feel alone, frightened, and unsafe.

Holding on to our opinions keeps us from seeing that life and other people are the way they are and are not affected by our opinions of how they should be.

It is a rude awakening to let go and accept life as it is, and that brings us to the last part of this book.

It is pointless to try to stop expecting.

Our wounded child inside expects.

That is just how he or she is and will always be.

It is a big part of our emotional child.

But we can transcend expectations by noticing them and going deeper inside to explore the fears and insecurities that lie behind them.

We can stop believing that the other person should meet those expectations.

Then the expectations start to drop away by themselves, and slowly we begin to see and accept people and life as they are.

Exercise: Exploring Your Expectations

Write down your answers that finish these two sentences:

"A good mother is one who…"

"A good father is one who…"

Notice in what ways your parents did not meet what you wrote.

Now take a moment to write down your answer to finish the next sentence:

"A loving partner is one who…"

For instance:

1. I expect that the person be present and available for me.

2. I expect that the person is considerate and listens to me.

3. I expect that the person is sensitive to my limits, perhaps even without my having to say anything.

4. I expect that the person provides for me financially.

5. I expect that the person touches me sensitively.

6. I expect that the person doesn't control or manipulate me for his or her own needs and wants.

7. I expect that the person is in his or her energy and not collapsed or indecisive.

8. I expect that the person does not expect me to rescue him or her.

9. I expect that the person works on himself or herself and is not in a state of denial about his feelings.

10. I expect that the person is meditative and conscious in how he or she lives (living space, care of the body etc.).

11. I expect that the person is sensitive and supportive of my creativity and spiritual growth.

Consider how the partner you have or have had compares to what you wrote.

Compare what you wrote about how your partner behaves or behaved to what you consider to be a good parent.

Compare how your partner to your mother and father.

Finally, take a moment to explore how you feel and act when he or she does not live up to your expectations.

CHAPTER 12:

CONTAINMENT

Rebecca cannot bear it when her boyfriend spends so much time at work and is not available to spend more time with her. She hates it when he chooses to go to play golf instead of spending time with her.

Catherine is suffering terribly because she has been left by her husband for another woman. She tells us, "I can't stand the pain. It is unbearable! There is no point in going on living without him. I have no life without him."

Although these situations are very different, both women are being challenged to learn how to contain their pain and frustration.

Our experiences of rejection challenge us to learn containment.

Containment means the ability to hold painful and disturbing feelings inside rather than acting out or in or denying them.

This is not the same as repression.

Repression is when we deny, avoid, or push down a painful or disturbing feeling or emotion because we are afraid to feel it.

Repression is swallowing the feelings.

Containment means giving room inside for the experience to open deeper spaces inside—to become bigger.

We learned to repress our feelings because it was not safe to feel them.

We might have been punished, beaten, rejected, or humiliated for feeling or expressing feelings which our parents, teachers, religion, or society in general found unacceptable.

We also learned to repress our feelings because we were not encouraged or supported in feeling some emotions such as anger, wildness, sadness, or fear, which our caregivers found uncomfortable or not important.

But worst of all, most of us did not have good modeling for how to be with fear and pain.

Many of us had parents who escaped their painful feelings with addictions, drama, or denial.

So we did not learn how stay present and accept pain.

Now in our lives, we are being challenged to learn this new skill.

That skill is to feel whatever feelings we have inside without either repressing them or acting out from them.

We call this *containment*.

It helps us to become mature and grounded.

It helps us become individuals.

Let's explore the process that helps us learn containment step-by-step:

Separating Feelings, Sensations, Thoughts, and Behavior

When we experience rejection, criticism, or being spoken to or treated disrespectfully, it provokes strong feelings inside.

This is the _trigger_.

The trigger provokes the following:

- There are the _feelings_—such as anger, sadness, shame, fear, or shock (frozenness).

- There are the _body sensations_ that the trigger provokes in the body.

- There are the _thoughts_ in the mind.

- And finally, there are the habitual, automatic, and often unconscious _behaviors_ that are provoked by the feelings and the thoughts.

Normally, when we are triggered, all of these aspects of our reaction to a disturbance run together and become confusing, overwhelming, and compulsive.

If we can take a moment to look closer at what is happening, to separate them, we can deal with them more easily.

Focusing on the body sensations

The secret of containment is to separate these aspects, become aware of them, and then to _focus on the sensations in the body_.

Let's take an example and come back to the situation with Rebecca.

When her boyfriend comes home from the office, she either yells at him or ignores him for coming home so late and threatens to leave him if he doesn't stop working so much. She doesn't take the time to notice the thoughts that are driving her emotions and her reactions, nor to focus on how his coming home late and how her negative thinking provoke sensations in her body.

Instead, she acts out compulsively and automatically.

When we ask how it feels that he is spending so much time at work and not giving her the time and attention she would like, she says,

"I don't know why I am with a man who has no time for me. I don't believe that he really loves me, or he would spend more time with me. I need to be with a man who really loves me."

Normally, when we are disturbed, our focus goes toward changing the situation or the other person.

Our negative thoughts about the other person and the situation take over.

We forget to notice the sensations in the body.

"Francesca," we asked, "when you examine your thoughts closely, is it really true that you think he doesn't love you?"

"No," she answered, "I think he does love me and he does want to spend time with me, but I get so frustrated and angry when I am always waiting for him. I feel rejected and I hate that feeling! In those moments, I doubt everything about our life together."

"OK," we suggested, "let's go back to the moment he comes home. He walks into the house. You have been waiting for him and you are feeling angry. Feel the sensations in your body as he comes in. Feel your chest; how does it feel? Is it tight?"

"My chest is tight, I feel tense in my belly, I am angry and I want to yell at him! I feel that I am never going to get what I want."

We said, "Well, actually that is a thought, but let's see how that thought makes you feel in your body."

She answered, "I feel anxious, I feel tighter in my chest. I feel heavy in my chest. I feel like crying. I feel that I don't deserve love; nobody will ever love me."

"OK," we said, "that last sentence is also a thought. How does that thought make you feel in your body? See if you can stay with the body feelings."

"I feel very sad." And she began to cry, and as the session progressed, she connected with memories of her mother giving attention to all her brothers and sisters (there were six children) and she felt she could never get enough attention from either of her parents.

As we kept helping her to stay with her body sensations, gradually she began to feel some relief, more space inside, and her body slowly relaxed.

"I notice when I stay with the body sensations, that I can let myself feel sad and that the heaviness gets lighter. I start to feel more space in my chest. I start to feel more relaxed. I can breathe now."

Our habit is to ignore our bodies and escape into acting out and believing our negative thoughts.

We can heal the shame and abandonment wounds by learning to stay focused on our bodies because it allows us to stay in the moment and observe our present here and now experience. And when we stay present and observe, gradually, we relax.

Most of us have the compelling belief that when we are disturbed, we have to act immediately to fix or change the situation.

This thought is a natural survival mechanism to help us feel safe and loved.

Unfortunately, in our daily lives and especially in our intimate relationships, trying to fix the outside situation—whether it is another person's behavior, the weather, or something else you are disturbed about—is not the solution to most problems.

And it is definitely not the way we can heal from our wounds of shame and abandonment.

By simply staying focused on the body sensations, something amazing happens.

The anxiety begins to decrease and we discover more energy and aliveness.

In this process of staying with the body, we also begin to see that the way of empowerment, inner peace, and self-love is not trying to change our environment or the other person.

Containment is the process of finding inner space to let life and other people be the way they are—and when things or other people are not how we would like them to be, to be willing to feel the frustration, anxiety, and fear that this brings up.

Framing

In order to find the space to deal with difficult moments in our lives— to deal with rejection—we need to find a new way of looking at and understanding those moments.

We need to find a positive interpretation so that we become motivated to deal with the fear and pain in a gentle way.

Imagine that you have to go to the doctor to get an injection.

You know that the injection will be painful, but you also know that you need to get it to get better.

You tell yourself, "I know that this is going to be painful, but it will make me feel better."

We can use the same kind of framing when we get rejected.

It is extremely helpful to know that all of these feelings are nothing more than the abandonment wound and the shame wound, and that we cannot heal what we are not willing to feel and understand.

When the pain is triggered today in our lives, it seems to our child inside that everything that happened in the past is happening right now. He or she cannot distinguish past from present.

But we are no longer a child and we now have the resources to heal.

Here is an affirmation to say to ourselves that might help:

"I know that this is a very painful time, but I also know that I can grow emotionally and spiritually from this experience. I know that by growing, it will improve all my relationships now and in the future. I know that I have the ability to deal with this pain even if at times it feels overwhelming. I know that feeling this pain helps me become more mature and to make different and healthier choices in the future."

When we frame an experience in a positive way, it allows us to go through the pain.

Pain is intolerable if it doesn't make any sense or have any meaning.

Finding Inner Space

Inner space is the sense that we can handle the ups and downs of life, knowing that we are capable of feeling any feeling that may come.

That sense comes when we realize that life is not always easy, and frequently we have to deal with difficult challenges that test us.

Taking deep conscious breaths is the medicine for giving us inner space.

Fear is the worst part of any difficult life experience.

Pain without fear is actually sweet.

But when there is fear, and when our minds begin to run with negative thoughts, our whole nervous systems get activated, disturbed, and agitated.

Sometimes just two or three deep breaths are enough to give us some distance from the fear and the pain.

But other times, nothing we can do will take away the anxiety.

In those moments we need to learn to be with it, give it time, and consciously not pay attention to the negative thoughts that tell us that it is too much, it will never go away, and nothing will ever change.

For instance, Charlotte says that she is tormented by her anxiety that arises unexpectedly. "It is too much," she tells us, "I can't stand it. What can I do?"

"We would suggest that you begin by using different words to describe what is happening. Instead of 'it is too much,' try, 'it is very strong.' And instead of 'I can't stand it,' try, 'I can learn to be with this fear and panic.'"

The words we use to describe our inner experiences have a strong influence on how we deal with them.

Then we gently guide her to feel her little girl inside that is taken over by fear in this moment, and we use the prop of her holding a pillow to help her take a little distance from the fear.

Then we suggest, "See if you can sense that there is another bigger and older part of you that has more space to just allow the fear. Allow yourself to hold that pillow and imagine that you are holding a small, innocent, and helpless child. Allow your breath and your love to soothe her fears."

This is just a brief summary of the method we use to help create inner space for our panic. We offer a more in-depth exploration on the meditation CD that is a partner to this book.

With time, Charlotte began to relax and feel more peace inside.

At first, it is helpful to have some guidance for us to learn inner space.

But after a while, we can manage to do it for ourselves.

Life brings us encounters with our wound of abandonment and rejection all the time, whether we like it or not.

They come in big or small doses and in different ways.

It may come when a lover leaves us or when a loved one dies.

It can happen when whatever was providing meaning in our lives no longer does, or whenever we are not getting what we want, expect, or think that we need from someone.

Whenever we have these experiences, we enter into a gap.

It is a space inside that has always been there but is usually covered with compensations, distractions, defenses, and denial.

When it finally opens, it can be frustrating, irritating, disappointing, or devastating.

These experiences are an invitation to take a step toward integration, maturity, and self-love by our finding the inner space inside to be with them and allow them to move through us.

Exercise 1: Meditation on the Five Aspects of Rejection

When you experience a rejection from someone—anyone—consider the following five aspects:

1. What is the *trigger*, what has the person done or not done, said or not said, that provoked you to feel rejected?

2. What are the *feelings* that are provoked?—sadness, hurt, anger, shame, or shock.

3. What are your *body sensations* that this experience is provoking inside you?—tightness in your chest or belly, stiff neck or shoulders, sweating, confusion, low energy.

4. What are your *negative thoughts*?—"He or she is..." "I am..." "Life is..." "People are..."

5. What are the ways that you *react* when this happens?—attack, blame,, withdraw, take revenge, punish, beg, deny, pretend it doesn't hurt, drink, smoke, eat, go shopping.

Exercise 2: Framing

When you experience a rejection or loss, allow yourself to reframe the experience by changing your negative thoughts to positive ones, such as:

- "This experience is giving me an important opportunity to grow."

- "The relationship was not going to work out in the long run, but I am learning tools to create a better one next time."

- "This experience has motivated me to reach out for help and guidance so that I can become a wiser, more mature, and integrated person."

Exercise 3: Developing Inner Space

The next time you notice yourself disturbed by feelings of rejection, feeling ignored, or feeling unloved, stop and take three deep breaths.

Then notice if you have more space inside.

CHAPTER 13:

ACCEPTANCE

It takes every resource we have to get through a rejection or abandonment experience.

And it hurts terribly when we discover that the person we have opened to is not the one we thought he or she was.

It hurts when we discover he or she has qualities or behaves in some ways that seem intolerable to us.

How can we make peace with these painful situations?

Acceptance comes:

When we understand why life has brought us a painful experience.

When we have the inner space to contain the pain.

And when we can find ways to learn from the experience.

Actually, rejection and abandonment are amazing gifts in disguise.

Of course, they don't seem like that at first, both because the experience is so painful and because usually we don't become aware of the gifts until later.

But let's take a look at why they are gifts.

1. *Pain forces us to grow*

As difficult as it is to accept pain when it arises in our lives, it is important to know that pain forces us to grow.

Why is this so?

- First of all, it gets our attention, wakes us up, and forces us to re-examine our lives as we have known them.

- Secondly, the process in itself of going through pain transforms us. It makes us deeper, wiser, and more compassionate. It brings us new insights about life and about ourselves.

- Thirdly, because the pain can be so intense, it inspires us to seek help where we can learn more about life and about ourselves.

- Finally, it strengthens our self-esteem because we know that we have been able to get through very difficult times and we have grown from it.

2. *Abandonment teaches us that pain and loss are parts of love*

Our deepest relationships will bring us face-to-face with our fears of rejection and loss.

The closer we come to someone, the deeper the hurt will be if we get rejected or if (and when) we lose the person.

Love includes the pain of loss and disappointment.

3. *Facing and accepting rejection and abandonment helps us to grow up*

The abandonment wound is inside of us and it was there long before we entered into our current relationships.

It needs to heal, and the only way it can heal is by being opened.

Rejection and abandonment break us open.

The biggest difference between being in the consciousness of a child or the consciousness of a mature adult is knowing that love brings us face-to-face with our abandonment wounds.

4. *Facing abandonment and rejection can be a deep spiritual opening*

While one part of our consciousness pushes away the fear and pain of rejection and abandonment as hard as it can, our higher consciousness welcomes it because it knows that in this experience lie great hidden treasures:

- The knowledge and power that no one on the outside can fill our holes inside.

- The knowledge and power that feeling the emptiness that abandonment brings up is the door to our deeper selves.

- The awareness that once we have found the ability to face our loneliness, it transforms into a deep inner peacefulness.

- The understanding that harmony in love comes when we no longer need the other person to take away our fear and our pain.

- The understanding that on a high level of our consciousness, we actually create abandonment crises to take us deeper.

As seekers of truth, the experience of abandonment gives us a totally new perspective. To our child, it is abandonment, but to our seeker, it is an entrance into a void that we all have to face sooner or later. Facing it can open a deep space of trust and the beginning to surrender.

5. Rejection is existence's way of protecting us

We seldom know at the time that very often when we get rejected, it is existence's way of protecting us from a dysfunctional situation.

If someone were to whisper that in your ear at the time the rejection happened, you would probably disagree.

But it's true.

Peter, from an earlier example, understood after several months that he was fortunate to be out of the relationship. If she had not ended it, he would most probably not have found the insight or the courage to do so and they might have continued to suffer in the relationship for a long time.

An Exercise of Acceptance

We offer a simple exercise to help us accept the pain of rejection or abandonment, and also the pain of any situation over which we have no control.

We can face these situations either with a closed fist, or an open palm.

When our fist is closed, we are resisting the pain; we are fighting with the experience and with life.

When our palm is open, we are in a gesture of surrender.

Imagine the last time you faced a situation that was painful.

Think of this situation and imagine it is happening at this moment.

Close your fists and feel the energy that your hands are expressing.

Give this energy a voice.

"I can't stand that this is happening."

"I hate this person for doing this to me!"

"How can life/God be so unjust and so unkind?"

"This pain is too much; I want it to go away."

Now, taking three deep breaths allowing your fists to slowly open; let the palms face upwards.

Relax your arms and hands and breathe into your heart.

Feel the energy of this position of your hands.

Give a voice to this energy.

For example: "I say yes to this pain, even though it hurts and I feel so helpless."

"I surrender to life."

"I let go of my struggle to control things."

"I will allow myself to feel the pain and the fears inside and relax into them."

CONCLUSION:

RECOVERING TRUST

We are born in an exquisite state of innocence and trust.

But all that changes—for one reason or another.

As we grow older, both our innocence and our trust gets damaged, often to the point where we begin to live in fear and mistrust.

We may even stop valuing ourselves or life itself.

It is our life's journey to recover that trust.

One of the principal ways that we can do that is to grow through experiences of rejection, abandonment, and loss.

These experiences test us.

They inspire us to discover what is real and what is true.

Deep inside, each one of us has the clear knowing that life and love are abundant.

This truth can be covered with many experiences, beginning in our childhoods that taught us the opposite.

When rejection or loss strikes, we have a choice.

Either we sink into anger, bitterness, resignation, and depression.

Or we use these experiences to find a deeper truth.

By using the tools outlined in this little book, we can do that.

Here are some of the tools and understandings that we recommend to help you with the pain and experience of abandonment and to make the transition from sinking into negativity to rising to truth.

1. Recognize that these experiences are perhaps the most painful and challenging experiences that you will ever have to face, and they take time to heal.

2. Seek out help from friends and a skilled person when you are dealing with the pain and confusion of rejection or abandonment.

3. Know that the pain of today is just the tip of the iceberg for the much deeper pain from multiple earlier experiences of neglect, abandonment, and lack of support for your basic needs.

4. With help, make the connection between the past and the present, and feel how the pain of today is much the same as what you may have felt in the past. This is deeply healing.

5. Know that the ongoing experiences of neglect, abandonment, and rejection can be deeply frustrating. Use these experiences to deepen yourself and take you on the road to maturity and peace, and to find more inner space.

6. Know that rejection is a hidden gift, both protecting you from unhealthy situations and guiding you to deeper understanding and love.

7. Remember to breathe when you are in pain and fear, remember that it will pass, and remember to tell yourself that you are growing with the pain.

Fundamentally, we all have a deep longing inside to be filled, to be whole.

The pain of abandonment and deprivation opens this deep longing.

That longing is the deepest part of our beings, because we are longing to return to the source.

It is at the heart of our spiritual search and mistakenly gets directed to other people.

We often feel the longing as a frightening loneliness, but this loneliness is a period of transition between feeling this loneliness and eventually coming to enjoy our aloneness, and rediscovering inner bliss and trust in life.

Instead of feeling universal love and a mystical sense of place and purpose in life, what comes at first, usually, are waves of intense heaviness and darkness.

Had we not suffered abandonment as children, this probably would not happen.

But we did, and so we have to go through this transition period.

It hurts and every part of our conscious minds wants to avoid feeling the pain.

Until we are willing to face these wounds, we meet pain, disappointment, and frustration with anger and expectation.

Then our journey through life cannot be deep or blissful, and our relationships will develop into superficial arrangements covering mountains of resentment.

Once we accept rejection and abandonment as an invitation to move into our depth, we are on our way home.

With love, Krishnananda and Amana

SELECTED REFERENCES

Krishnananda Trobe, M.D. with Amana Trobe, *Face to Face with Fear—Transforming Fear into Love (Revised Edition)* Perfect Publisher LMD, Cambridge, England 2009

Krishnananda Trobe, M.D. and Amana Trobe, *From Fantasy Trust to Real Trust, Learning from Our Disappointments and Betrayals, (Revised Edition)* The Learning Love Institute, Sedona, AZ 2011

Pia Mellody, *The Intimacy Factor—The Ground Rules for Overcoming the Obstacles to Truth, Respect, and Lasting Love,* Harper San Francisco, 2004

Susan Anderson, *The Journey from Abandonment to Healing—Surviving through and Recovering from the Five Stages that Accompany the Loss of Love,* Berkeley Books, New York, N.Y. 2000

Janea B. Weinhold, PhD and Barry K. Weinhold, PhD, *The Flight from Intimacy: Healing Your Relationship of Counter-dependency—the Other Side of Co-dependency,* New World Library, Novato, CA 2009

John Bradshaw, *Creating Love—The Next Stage of Growth,* Bantam Books, New York, N.Y. 1994

Made in the USA
Lexington, KY
17 September 2019